ADVANCE PRAISE FOR

Beyond Compensation:

Empowering Teachers' Unions to Think Beyond Bread-and-Butter Issues

"*Beyond Compensation: Empowering Teachers' Unions to Think Beyond Bread-and-Butter Issues*, chronicles two decades of work by Terence Ngwa and the Washington Teachers Union to improve education for DC's children while also advocating for the teachers who are his union's members. Grounded in such union initiatives as community schools, annual "Shared Vision Conferences, and DC Council hearings, such a chronicle means running into the ever-complicated world of Washington, DC education: mayoral control; ever-changing mayoral-appointed Chancellors, starting with Michelle Rhee; and the huge charter school sector, imposed on DC by Newt Gingrich's Congress. The book's story belies the stereotype of teacher unions as just self-interested."

—Ruth Wattenberg,
Former President,
DC State Board of Education

"Dr. Ngwa's latest book, *Beyond Compensation: Empowering Teachers' Unions to Think Beyond Bread-and-Butter Issues*, is essential reading for anyone interested in making sure that American schools provide excellent educational opportunities to all students."

—Larry Rubin,
former speechwriter,
US Department of Education

"In clearly delineated chapters, Terence Ngwa, in *Beyond Compensation: Empowering Teachers' Unions to Think Beyond Bread-and-Butter Issues*, offers clear thinking on how we can improve our school system. His research is experience-based and pragmatic, based on both his classroom and union experience. He offers the steps unions should take to enhance the education of all our students."

—Alice Heiserman,
former teacher,
President, WriteBooksRight

I0807765

"Dr. Ngwa's *Beyond Compensation: Empowering Teachers' Unions to Think Beyond Bread-and-Butter Issues* is a powerful and timely examination of teachers' unions as champions of social justice, educational equity, and democratic values. Ngwa dismantles the narrative that unions merely protect self-interest and offers a well-researched perspective that positions them as vital advocates for students, families, and communities—particularly those historically marginalized by our education system. At a moment when public education faces unprecedented threats, Dr. Ngwa reminds us of the importance of educators' unions in the coalition fighting for equity and justice in our schools."

—kecia hayes,
PhD - American University

Beyond Compensation

The Badass Teachers Association Education Book Series

Brianne Kramer and Melissa Tomlinson, Editors

In the spirit of the **Badass Teachers Association**, this book series aims to develop a forum for current practitioners and researchers to publish works dedicated to the activism, advocacy, and profession-building work P-16 faculty conduct within their schools and communities to preserve the common good and create equitable learning environments centered in social justice principles. The **Badass Teachers Association** Education book series is rooted in the original mission of the organization, which "reject[s] racially and socially oppressive profit-driven education reform."

This book series serves to contribute to educators' and educational leaders' understandings of the need for teacher education, activism, and leadership in these areas. It will provide a place for future and current educators to learn more about these issues and how they can build their classrooms and communities into the spaces all students deserve. This series will consist of print books and e-books for current educators, pre-service teachers, parents, and others in the greater community.

New and Forthcoming Titles

The Critical Importance of Teacher Advocacy:
Empowerment, Activism, and the Goal of Improving Our Public Schools
by Melissa Tomlinson and Brianne Kramer (2026)

Beyond Compensation:
Empowering Teachers' Unions to Think Beyond Bread-and-Butter Issues
by Terence Ngwa (2026)

Learning From Teachers During COVID:
Recommendations for Strengthening the Teaching Profession
by Denisha Jones, Clint Broadbent, and Brianne Kramer (2026)

If you have a proposal for this series, we welcome your submission. Please send your prospectus and CV to the series editors, Brianne Kramer (briannekramer@suu.edu) or Melissa Tomlinson (contact.batmanager@gmail.com).

Beyond Compensation

Empowering Teachers' Unions to Think Beyond Bread-and-Butter Issues

BY Terence Ngwa

Myers Education Press

Gorham, Maine

Myers Education Press

Published by Myers Education Press, LLC
P.O. Box 424
Gorham, ME 04038

Myers Education Press is an academic publisher specializing in books, e-books, and digital content in the field of education. All of our books are subjected to a rigorous peer review process and produced in compliance with the standards of the Council on Library and Information Resources.

Library of Congress Cataloging-in-Publication Data available from Library of Congress.

13-digit ISBN 978-1-9755-0767-1 (paperback)
13-digit ISBN 978-1-9755-0768-8 (library networkable e-edition)
13-digit ISBN 978-1-9755-0769-5 (consumer e-edition)

Printed in the United States of America.

All first editions printed on acid-free paper that meets the American National Standards Institute Z39-48 standard.

Books published by Myers Education Press may be purchased at special quantity discount rates for groups, workshops, training organizations, and classroom usage. Please call our customer service department at 1-800-232-0223 for details.

Cover design by Teresa Lagrange.
Istock credit: StockPlanets.

Visit us on the web at **www.myersedpress.com** to browse our complete list of titles.

DEDICATION

To Elizabeth Ann Davis of blessed memory

Three-term President of the Washington Teachers' Union

and

all the hardworking men and women

who have dedicated their lives to protecting

the rights of educators and doing what is right for students.

CONTENTS

ACKNOWLEDGMENTS

The challenges of writing as an art are enormous, but not insurmountable. Having the motivation and time to write, let alone finding the right words, can be as daunting as anyone would expect. Never in my wildest imagination did I think I would venture into spending these many hours and sleepless nights to write a book, but when you hang out in the company of the right people, the decision becomes seamless. When Alice Heiserman, president of Write Books Right, edited my doctoral dissertation, her instincts told her I could do more than just a doctoral dissertation, and she became my motivating force. When I was invited to serve on a panel at the Institute for International Education in Washington, D.C. following the ruling on the *Janus v. AFSCME* decision, Larry Rubin, Alice's partner, was working with me at the Washington Teachers' Union (WTU) as Communications Director. As Larry helped me with talking points for the panel, he and Alice encouraged me to develop some of the content into a book, and both of them were there to cheer me on as I debated and pushed back on anti-union rhetoric by one of the panelists. Alice continued to help with content editing and the search for potential publishers, and has worked tirelessly to ensure that this dream became a reality. I am incredibly grateful for Alice's and Larry's support throughout this journey.

Although I consider myself a union insider, I could not have developed some of the content on my own without the perspectives I obtained from rank-and-file members of the WTU. Their views and perspectives helped me develop some of the ideas shared in this book. I am extremely indebted to the president of the United Teachers of Dade, who in the midst of adversity in a very hostile environment in Florida could still make the time to grant me an interview. And of course, the union powerhouse, American Federation of Teachers' President Randi Weingarten played a very instrumental role in helping me process and deliver some of the content of my manuscript through her usual expert analysis of the union's role in a democracy, even after a disappointing loss in an election that she and her members invested in tremendously.

Finally, I learned how to write using a small tablet-size chalk board at a time when the dream of coming close to a typewriter was very remote, but here I am, many decades after my first encounter with a writing utensil, typing on a computer keyboard. I have never found words to appreciate the efforts of the person who laid that foundation, my aunt (mother), Mama Mary Bi. Without her, writing and publishing a book would never have occurred in my lifetime. The only way I can appreciate her efforts is by empowering my children, Terence Jr. and Kristine, with the gift of literacy. Both of them are developing formidable writing skills at their young ages. Thank you, Kristine, for writing along with me and being my accountability partner; I can't wait to read your manuscript when it is ready. Terry, your short story on the meaning of freedom sits on my office bookshelf as a reminder of how you distinguish yourself among your peers with your strong writing skills. And to my wife, Yvonne, thank you for the motivation and for creating the space for me to write.

FOREWORD

We editors are pleased to present *Beyond Compensation: Empowering Teachers' Unions to Think Beyond Bread-and-Butter Issues* as the first book in The Badass Teacher Education Book Series. This text emulates the aim of the series as it delves into the American Federation of Teachers Local and how educator unions have worked to make change within their schools and the communities they serve. Terence's personal experience in the Washington Teachers' Union adds a unique, empirical perspective to different pivotal moments throughout the recent history of public education in our country. We believe educators will find these anecdotes as potential models for what unions nationwide can accomplish.

Beyond Compensation gives an interesting overview of a time when educator unions were reconciling with the fact that they had to be more than associations of members and start building collective power to fight back against the corporatization of public education. This book takes us through the historical impacts of No Child Left Behind and other education reforms that followed, designed to disregard the voice of educators, the experts, in decision-making for public education. Terence provides the reader with a thorough account of how collaboration, inclusive of educator voice as one stakeholder, can create substantive positive change in communities. Collaboration between educators and administrators, union members and managers, serves as a potential launching point for education stakeholders to develop ways to push back against the divisiveness that has been used as a tool to dismantle education.

Today's educators find themselves in a precarious position, as they have been targeted by state and federal legislators and face daily challenges. Additionally, the COVID-19 pandemic as a global epidemic had a lasting impact on national and global support systems that were in place to maintain the status quo. These did not do anything to address the systemic issues in place that prevent access to complete human rights and dignities. Now under the pressure of the current Presidential administration, which seeks to eliminate protections for historically minoritized populations, there is an urgent need for educators to push back through unionization and advocacy. In this present time, unions need to consider new ways of organizing and utilizing their power as attacks levied at educational institutions from the far-Right and neoliberal movements continue to build.

Beyond Compensation provides many insights into the inner workings of a large educator union chapter, including a refreshing analysis of areas for improvement. This careful and vulnerable discussion of issues experienced within the organization is crucial to understanding how unions can improve to better serve their members and evolve past those "bread-and-butter" issues. As unions grow and leadership shifts, changes are inevitable. Terence takes care to discuss some constrictions experienced during these times of change and how they were remedied when opportunities allowed. Every organization experiences issues and hardships, and the text provides an opportunity for readers to think about their organizations' issues and potential solutions.

Overall, we hope readers engage with *Beyond Compensation* with their own unions and organizations in mind. As we all work to build collective power, the lived reality of one AFT chapter is a powerful case study for others to learn from and consider the potential for building past those bread-and-butter issues unions have generally organized around. We editors believe it vital at this point in time to think creatively about the potential each union or organization has in the fight to keep public education strong. Engage your colleagues and those around you to participate in this growing movement. Engage your communities in this fight for the public good. Attacks on unions will continue, potentially far past this current Presidential administration. Stay in the fight, as our livelihood depends on it.

In Solidarity,
The Badass Teachers Association Education Series Editors
Melissa Tomlinson
Brianne Kramer, Ph.D.

PREFACE

The idea to write *Beyond Compensation: Empowering Teachers' Unions to Think Beyond Bread-and-Butter Issues* was born out of my involvement in organized labor as a teacher in the District of Columbia Public Schools system. Over a period of 15 years, I worked my way up from being a rank and file member, activist, and elected to various roles in a school building, to serving on the executive board before accepting the position of executive director of the union.

The opportunities that teachers' unions have used to intensify their advocacy for issues that are more of the common good than their work on wages and working conditions gave me the inspiration to take a closer look at what research there is and what is being done in the local with which I worked closely. Even in areas where the focus was on working conditions such as smaller class sizes, the end goal remained the improvement of student outcomes through such demands for change. There is good evidence to believe that teachers enter the profession for reasons other than money, and even though they would like to earn a living wage and work under acceptable conditions, fighting for issues that matter to their students and their immediate communities has become front-and-center to what they do.

Around the country, in addition to the major teachers' unions and their affiliates, other advocacy groups that support their cause have emerged. Within the major teachers' unions themselves, different caucuses have sprouted to amplify critical workplace issues that affect the quality of learning for students and the teaching profession as a whole. AFT's Badass Teachers Association has taken a very active role in pushing an agenda that prioritizes a healthy workplace for educators and a learning environment that prioritizes the needs of all children. The Journey for Justice (J4J) alliance on its part has built a national alliance of parents and grassroots movements to protect and maintain the integrity of traditional public schools and to aggressively resist school privatization initiatives around the country. The organization's racial and social justice agenda has been embraced by teachers' unions through ongoing collaborative partnerships. These alliances and partnerships, as well as other examples of what teachers' unions represent, are highlighted in depth in *Beyond Compensation* as ways of demonstrating what K–12 educators have advocated for decades, which is demanding respect for the profession, affording each student regardless of zip code the right to a public education, and equitably investing resources in every school. Demanding a fair wage and good working conditions cannot be regarded in isolation, but rather as a condition that guarantees school environments where students are learning without distractions of any kind.

The ideas espoused in this book are based on extensive research spanning a period of six years, my personal experiences serving as a union member and leader for 18 years, interviews with union leaders, and my observations and interactions with leaders and allies at all levels, as well as with rank-and-file members of the Washington Teachers' Union and the American Federation of Teachers during my tenure as Executive Director from 2018–2021.

INTRODUCTION

Organized labor is the bedrock of every economy around the globe. Workers' rights are enshrined in the principles set forth by the International Labor Organization (ILO). The United States Department of Labor through its membership thus has an obligation to adhere to these principles which call for the respect, promotion of freedom of association, and the effective recognition of the right to collective bargaining; elimination of all forms of forced or compulsory labor; effective abolition of child labor; elimination of discrimination with respect to employment and occupation; and a safe and healthy working environment. U.S. workers benefit from additional protections through the Civil Rights Act of 1964 which protects employees and prospective employees from discrimination based on race, gender, color, sex, religion, or national origin. Employees have further protections under the National Labor Relations Board to join forces with or without a union to improve their wages and working conditions.

The fundamentals of what teachers' unions and other unions are involved in are an attempt to collectively advocate for better wages and working conditions. Unfortunately, in the course of engaging in practices that are universally sanctioned as human rights, workers are constantly susceptible to attacks by forces seeking to exploit their labor. Paying workers a fair wage and safeguarding their well-being through safe worksite conditions and fringe benefits do not amount to a handout from their respective employers.

The quest for fair and equitable working conditions has traditionally pushed workers to collectively organize to demand compensation that is up to par with the standard of living in their respective countries. In countries where collective bargaining is the norm, unions have been instrumental in demanding and acquiring their fair share of compensation, shaping public policy, and going as far as influencing elections in support of union-friendly candidates. In Europe, particularly in France, work stoppages have resulted in major slowdowns in economic activities at enormous costs to the population, and even travelers and tourists get caught in the crosshairs. The educational sector has been very instrumental in its collective bargaining efforts with massive support coming from both K–12 educators and the intelligentsia in higher education.

The United States of America has enjoyed the influence of two major teachers' unions—the National Education Association (NEA) with three million members (National Education Association, n.d.) and the American Federation of Teachers (AFT) with over 1.8 million (American Federation of Teachers, n.d.). Relations between the teachers' unions and school districts have historically been adversarial, typically characterized by strikes over working conditions and equitable pay. Because of these adversarial relationships, the early days of the labor movement were characterized by threats to union leaders through anti-strike injunctions that, when violated, resulted in stiff penalties such as fines, revocation or suspension of licenses, termination of employment, or jail time in some cases. At least 37 out of the 50 states in the U.S. do not allow teachers the right to strike. These adversarial relations were not peculiar to unions and management only, but a general animosity and hostility prevailed toward labor unions, especially from Right-leaning state governments. The passing of legislation such as the Right To Work (RTW) and counter protests and strikes by labor groups exacerbated the adversarial relations over time. The inability of labor and management to reach common ground on issues and on collaborative practices made their relationships over time untenable in some instances. In the case of teachers' unions, the ultimate victims were students and their families when teachers went on strike, forcing schools to close down. Teachers' unions have typically been sympathetic to Left-leaning politicians who have reciprocated such support which in turn has drawn the ire of anti-union states and groups. Like all unions around the country, the AFT in particular and its affiliates have not been immune to adversarial relationships with the respective school districts in which they operate even though nothing in their mission is antithetical to what families and communities desire—fairness, democracy, economic opportunity, high-quality public education, healthcare, and public services for students.

In the District of Columbia, where I served as an educator from 2003 to 2021, the mayoral takeover of the District of Columbia Public Schools (DCPS) from an elected school board in 2007 ushered in a new era of adversarial relationships between the teachers' union and the mayor's appointee for chancellor, Michelle Rhee. Top-down leadership, characterized by the non-involvement of the teachers' union in new initiatives such as teacher evaluation, professional development, and the choice of curriculum, provoked a call for more collaboration between the two entities—similar to the nationwide trend recommended by the parent organization—with the goal of benefitting students.

In the 1960s and 1970s, working conditions were the most contentious issues that led to severe strikes in the district and other jurisdictions. William (Bill) Simons, the first president of the Washington Teachers' Union (WTU), not only led the local to its first-ever collective bargaining agreement, but also led two successful strikes in 1972 and 1979 as well as a march on Capitol Hill to demand teacher pay raises. In recent years, the main threat that members of the union faced emanated from a teacher evaluation system that they deemed and continue to deem punitive, and rightfully so, due to the number of educators who have been separated from the system due to low scores.

In the early years of the Obama administration, the school district, like many around the country, sought to meet school reform exigencies proposed by the administration to improve public educational outcomes. Although school reform was embraced as a welcome move, educators around the country have argued that they will continue to doubt the credibility of some aspects of school reform such as merit-based and punitive evaluation systems and other initiatives that are based on a hierarchical system. These systems tend to be top-down with little or no room for teacher input (Sims, 2015).

Public education in the United States has always been in crisis, leading almost every administration in the White House in recent memory to attempt some type of education reform legislation to improve it. In the 1980s, education reform came into the spotlight with the landmark study *Nation at Risk* (Eberts, 2007). Since then, teachers and their unions have come under persistent scrutiny and attack by proponents of the education reform movement and policymakers. Accusations directed toward teachers' unions have included the following: the intentional slowdown of school reform initiatives, the prioritization of union interests, the protection of incompetent teachers, and the preoccupation of union agendas with job security over student outcomes. These accusations exacerbated historically adversarial relationships between labor unions and management, and specifically, the "us-versus-them" mentality between unions and school districts around the country, where both sides have sparingly worked together to improve student outcomes although the unions have pushed for increased collaboration.

The 2020 COVID-19 pandemic and social justice protests triggered by police brutality around the country marked the start of a new era of not only mistrust between teachers' unions and management, but also what some in the education community considered an outright attack on teachers. Parents advocating for their children to return to in-person learning in school environments that teachers considered unsafe, the banning of books that focus on the history of slavery and racism in the country, attacks on school board members for supporting social justice movements, and the attack on LGBTQ students all worsened existing problems in K–12 education, some of which resulted in the massive resignation of teachers in different jurisdictions around the country.

The unions, in turn, have continued to undercut the attacks on their members with a change in culture favoring a culture that shifts from the industrial unionism model to professional and social unionism. They have engaged in organizing efforts that focus on appealing to their members' sense of pride for their profession, social responsibility, and advocacy for students and their families. The AFT's *Reclaim the Promise* campaign (American Federation of Teachers, 2013) was part of the major shifts that amplified the values of what the organization espouses. One of its publications specifically targeted racial equity in education, economics, and the criminal justice system. The arguments on both sides presented a unique opportunity to determine if there was any value to short-term and long-term collaborative partnerships between the unions and management, or between teachers and school administrators.

Over the years, some teachers' unions have continued to be more progressive by initiating collaboration with management rather than pushing an agenda that could be deemed adversarial or combative. The Washington Teachers' Union (WTU), for example, inspired by changes in culture among other AFT affiliates, and in line with the social justice philosophy of its founding president, began to intentionally include language in its collective bargaining agreements (CBAs) that called for full and equal partnership with management. In their most recent CBAs, District of Columbia Public Schools (DCPS) and WTU agreed to work collaboratively through the Full and Equal Partnership provision and a Memorandum of Agreement (MOA) to collaboratively form a climate curriculum taskforce. Although some success was achieved around joint trainings on the implementation of the agreement and professional development, some areas such as teacher induction and mentoring have never been implemented. The school district, however, has argued that its coaching model called LIFT serves as a mentoring program despite the fact that there is no collaboration with the union. Rather than constantly oppose management, teachers' unions have sought a solution-driven approach to dealing with areas of contention with management. Other models of collaboration abound nationwide, notably in Hillsborough County, Florida Public Schools (HCPS); ABC Unified School District (ABCUSD), California; Jefferson County Public Schools, Colorado; and Montgomery County Public Schools (MCPS), to name a few (Rubinstein et al., 2011).

Further Reading

American Federation of Teachers. (n.d.). *About Us.* https://www.aft.org/about

American Federation of Teachers. (2013). *Reclaiming the promise of public education* [Resolution]. https://www.aft.org/resolution/reclaiming-promise-public-education

Brogan, P. (2016). Education deform and social justice unionism. *Labour / Le Travail, 77*, 225–241.

Collective Bargaining Agreement, Washington Teachers' Union-District of Columbia Public Schools, 2016–2019.

Coulson, A. J. (2010). The effects of teachers' unions on American education. *CATO Journal, 30*(1), 155–170.

Eberts, R. W. (2007). Teachers unions and student performance: Help or hindrance? *Future of Children, 17*(1), 175–200.

Kirp, D. L. (2014). Banding together: Union City's teachers and administrators work together to improve student achievement. *American Educator, 37*(4), 14–21.

Mirer, J. (2013). Right-to-work laws: History and fightback. *National Lawyers Guild Review, 70*(1), 30–40.

National Education Association. (n.d.). Mission, vision & values. https://www.nea.org/about-nea/mission-vision-values

Rubinstein, S. A., McCarthy, J. E., & Center for American Progress. (2011). *Reforming public school systems through sustained union-management collaboration.* Center for American Progress.

Shelton, J. (2014). Letters to the Essex County penitentiary: David Selden and the fracturing of America. *Journal of Social History, 48*(1), 135–155.

Simon, M. (2012). A tale of two districts. *Educational Leadership, 70*(3), 58–63.

Sims, M. L. (2015). The business of teaching: Can a new contract change the culture? *Columbia Journal of Law & Social Problems, 48*(4), 605–652.

Sustar, L. (2013). Teachers' unions at the crossroads: Can the assault on teachers be rebuffed? *New Labor Forum (Sage Publications Inc.), 22*(2), 60–68. https://doi.org/10.1177/10957

Tucker, M. (2012). A different role for teachers' unions? *Education Digest, 77*(9), 4–10.

Vachon, T. E., & Ma, J. (Kuo-H. (2015). Bargaining for success: Examining the relationship between teacher unions and student achievement. *Sociological Forum, 30*(2), 391–414. https://doi.org/10.1111/socf.12168

CHAPTER 1

We Care

Caring means being present, fully attentive, and genuinely interested in the well-being of others.

— Thich Nhat Hanh

The recurring question at many teacher recruitment fairs and interviews revolves around the reasons why the candidate chose to enter the profession. Candidates have wasted no time in providing the obvious answer without flinching, which is "because I care about children." That care, although clichéd, is reflected in the everyday work that educators do in schools. It is in addition to the obvious day-to-day tasks which involve preparing and leading academic content, addressing the social-emotional needs of students, and serving as student advocates—all priorities for educators. The various unions have amplified these elements of care and publicly demanded respect for the profession and respect for the professionals who serve the students, especially those in underserved communities. In recent years, more than in historical memory, teachers' unions have taken on social justice as a key facet of their vision among the many other issues they fight for. Educators come to work every day, pushing for equity and safety for all students, especially minority and other vulnerable groups of students. While school districts have prioritized some of these issues, local and national teachers' unions are the loudest voices for measures to close the racial achievement and opportunity gaps in education.

Unions' push for equity and safety has attracted allies and partners through a multiplicity of initiatives aimed at leveling the playing field for all students regardless of race, national origin, immigration status, ethnicity, economic status, gender, sexual orientation, or zip code. Teachers' unions build bridges to opportunity for all students.

Gun Violence

Figure 1.1 AFT 2018 Gun Violence Resolution

Press Release

AFT Executive Council Condemns Gun Violence

For Release:
Wednesday, February 21, 2018

Contact:
Andrew Crook
o: 202-393-8637 | c: 607-280-6603
acrook@aft.org

WASHINGTON—At a meeting of its executive council today, the American Federation of Teachers passed a wide-ranging resolution condemning gun violence and calls to arm teachers, while urging action to protect children and educators from gun violence. AFT President Randi Weingarten said:

"It's time for politicians to value children over the gun lobby. AFT members will not rest until we prevent military-style weapons from getting into the hands of people who want to massacre children and educators. And if our current elected officials won't change the laws to protect our kids and create safe schools, we'll change who gets elected in November.

"I am in awe of the students who are leading right now—and their educators. These are kids who sheltered in closets, who lost their friends, who wrote texts to their families thinking they had one last opportunity to say they loved them, who took a bullet for each other, or who witnessed a killing field. The students, supported by their teachers, are speaking out the loudest, organizing on social media and in their schools, and they are determined to turn this moment into a movement.

"I am sickened by those doing the bidding of the gun lobby, and those like President Trump and Betsy DeVos who want an arms race and to turn schools into militarized fortresses by arming teachers. Anyone who wants guns in schools has no understanding of what goes on inside them—or worse, doesn't care. And how dare anyone, especially the president's son, endorse the sick online attacks on the students of Stoneman Douglas? These are kids who experienced huge trauma and are fighting for their lives, and the lives of others.

"Today, our union rededicated ourselves to doing everything we can to protect kids and educators and prevent gun violence in our schools. We support every action being organized. We will be with you in the streets, in our statehouses, in Washington and at the ballot box. We are joining with teachers, students, parents and communities for a national day of action on April 20, the anniversary of the Columbine shooting, to stop gun violence in our schools. We are coming together with those who learn in, teach in, send their kids to and care about public schools, to take a stand."

The AFT and the National Education Association (NEA) and their affiliates are on the frontlines, aggressively seeking measures that guarantee student safety, especially in the wake of mass shootings and neighborhood gun violence around the country. Actions geared at curbing gun violence in schools have included the AFT's National Day of Action against gun violence in schools, walkouts, lesson plans for educators, and active participation in the March for Our Lives, among other actions. Gun legislation has been and still is a politically polarizing issue on which unions have taken an active advocacy role. Such a position does not benefit the rank and file financially, nor does it add to other fringe benefits that they have promoted over the years, but rather focuses on the well-being of students and the communities they live in.

The teachers' positions on gun violence focus solely on the safety and emotional well-being of the students that they serve. Nothing stabs a teacher more in the gut than attending the funeral of a former or current student or dealing with the emotions of an elementary, middle, or high school student dealing with grief following the senseless death of a family member from gun violence. No matter the circumstances, teachers have the responsibility to both deal with a bereaved student's trauma, while at the same time teach the curriculum and hold the same student accountable for successful outcomes. The pressure to deliver on student outcomes is further exacerbated by standardized testing mandates imposed on teachers to ensure that their students are performing at an acceptable level. Advocacy for what is right for children's safety therefore is an area of priority, closely related to what teachers' unions fight for in their daily efforts.

In response to schools' mass shootings, pro-gun groups and lawmakers have called for teachers to be armed as a way of defending their students from gun violence. Such measures, the unions argue, would divert much-needed funds, which could have been allocated to fund necessary school programs, to the gun industry to increase their profit margins. Amid the entire safety debate about keeping students safe, teachers are not asking for shields from bullets at their jobsites; they are shielding students with their bodies. Stories of teachers hiding their students in supply closets in response to a gunman in their building or being brutally slaughtered or wounded in an attempt to protect their students have become prevalent in American schools.

After the mass shooting in an El Paso, Texas Walmart on August 3, 2019 that left 22 students dead, just four days after another shooting at a Mississippi Walmart that left two employees dead, President of the American Federation of Teachers (AFT) Randi Weingarten went the extra mile to launch an outright attack on Walmart for its sale of arms and ammunition. Randi's threat on behalf of her members to boycott Walmart for its gun sales and donations to lawmakers who were standing in the way of gun reform added to the pressure on the retail giant to take immediate action. Notably, Walmart agreed to discontinue the sale of certain types of ammunition and to prohibit customers, with the exception of law enforcement officers, from openly carrying firearms in its stores nationwide. Even though the changes did not go as far as the second largest teachers' union in the country had wished, it was a step in the right direction. The pressure that the teachers' union and other groups mounted left Walmart with no option other than to act in this direction (Meyersohn, 2019).

For many years, teachers, students, and their communities held vigils for students who were victims of gun violence, yet no one has found a real solution to the problem. After the infamous shooting at Sandy Hook Elementary School in Newtown, Connecticut in December 2012 that left 26 dead, 17 at Stoneman Douglas High School in Parkland, Florida in February 2018, and 19 students and two teachers in Uvalde, Texas, teachers organized around protecting their students. Several gun violence events and marches were organized in local jurisdictions to bring attention to and call for action around the issue. In August 2018, Hailey Snow, a consultant with the AFT, approached the leadership of the WTU to collaborate on a planned gun violence summit in October, potentially at a D.C. school—the main organizer was AFT member Abby Clements, who was a second-grade teacher at Sandy Hook at the time of the shooting. As executive director of the local teachers' union at the time, my assistance in securing Dunbar Senior High School to host the summit was invaluable. The choice of Washington, D.C. was not a coincidence given its own history of almost weekly gun violence that affected students directly and indirectly. The summit brought together students and teachers from around the country to push for tougher gun laws (Reeve, 2018).

At the culmination of the two-day summit, students passed a School Safety Bill of Rights to be presented to lawmakers. Becky Miller, a social studies teacher at Eastern Senior High School in Washington, D.C., as quoted by WJLA News, believed that "Kids are dying in the schools to a point where it's not even a lead news story anymore" (Reeve, 2018, p. 1). Yet not long after the summit, another student was shot at Anacostia Senior High School, and his schoolmate, Thomas Johnson, became the next victim in October 2019.

In both cases and numerous others, the local union president at the same time, a longtime resident of Washington, D.C., sent condolences to her affected members and their communities to demonstrate sympathy for what the community was enduring.

After Johnson's murder and the message that WTU President Elizabeth Davis sent to her members at Anacostia, I suggested that the local union organize a D.C. Student Gun Violence Summit. Coincidentally, Joe Weedon, a former D.C. State Board of Education (SBOE) representative and parent had joined the union as Communications Specialist. In addition to his communications portfolio, Joe would also help with advocacy and the policy agenda of the union, given his expertise and background as a former member of the SBOE. Even though Joe agreed to take the lead on the planned gun violence prevention event, we also solicited logistical support from our parent organization, the AFT. After meeting with Hailey Snow and Earl Hadley, Assistant Director of Legislation at AFT, we decided to schedule a conference call with Abby Clements and other staff of AFT Communications to assist in planning the event. As time went on, it became evident that the event would garner more support with the involvement of other grassroots organizations that had been involved in fighting gun violence in the city. The idea of another meeting was thus born, only this time, it involved other groups. Moms Demand Action, the D.C. YMCA, MIKVA, Global Kids, Serve Your City, the Office of the Attorney General, and some members of Anacostia Senior High School staff met with the organizing staff at the WTU on December 19, 2019 to plan a future event that was tentatively set for January 16, 2020 before the Martin Luther King Junior holiday weekend.

As January 16 approached, it had become clear that the group could not pull together a summit, but believed a rally and press conference would suffice to bring attention to the student demands that the coalition planned to help them make to city legislators. In spite of pushback from our partners at the AFT that the event wasn't ready, and concerns that they would not have time to secure media, the turnout was surprisingly impressive, and local media outlets, including a French local media house that received the press advisory through one of the local union's partners, showed up.

In addition to using student demands to help curb gun violence in the city, the local union also used its advocacy around equitable school funding to demand that the mayor's school budget allocate $14 million to expand services from 119 schools to 159 schools and $10.6 million to ensure every school could offer high-quality, evidence-based social-emotional learning programs and trauma-informed training. The union also called for a $25 million investment in before and after school, as well as summer programming.

Social Justice

In the District of Columbia, the Washington Teachers' Union (WTU), an affiliate of the AFT, has touted its efforts around social justice as the center of its work, especially under the leadership of its former president Elizabeth Davis. The local's push for equity for all students has been and continues to be relentless. The former leader described herself as a social justice, solution-driven leader, and it is evident from the local's messaging that her legacy, although not explicitly articulated by the current leadership, is in its social justice agenda.

Social justice has always been at the core of the local's organizing, even at a time when the focus appeared to be solely on obtaining protections for members. That was the case in the 1970s when the local president, Bill Simons, led a strike in violation of city law. Although the union was hit with a monetary fine for such a violation, Mr. Simons was able to convince the judge to allocate the fine toward a scholarship fund to benefit the predominantly Black student population to become teachers. At the time of Simons' death, many Black students had benefited from the fund and are currently serving as teachers. Today, the fund partially supports D.C. public schools' students pursuing a degree in Education at the American University School of Education.

In addition to its diversity, the District of Columbia faces social inequities in its residents' incomes, and disparities in housing, healthcare, and education funding similar to those in inner cities around the country such as in Philadelphia, Baltimore City, Chicago, and Los Angeles. These inequities create a clear path for the teachers' union in D.C. to position itself as a voice for the student population and their families. Such advocacy was very prevalent during the

COVID-19 pandemic. The union's advocacy for social justice dates back to the 1960s. It is no surprise that the union's first Collective Bargaining Agreement (CBA) with the school district, ratified in 1968, set the tone for matters related to social justice.

In the 1968 CBA, the union and the school district agreed on the racial integration of both staff and students and fair employment practices for all, regardless of race, creed, color, national origin, sex, or marital status. They also mutually agreed to investigate outcomes for students through racial integration. Although the Supreme Court ruled in *Brown v. Board of Education* in 1954 that racial segregation in public schools was unconstitutional, some vestiges still abounded in the District of Columbia in the 1960s, with schools such as Jackson-Reed (formerly Wilson) Senior High School only beginning their integration process after *Hobson v. Hansen* in 1967, which challenged the District of Columbia's Board of Education regarding racial inequities in educational opportunities (*Hobson v. Hansen, 1967*).

Specifically, civil rights activist Julius Hobson charged Superintendent Carl Hansen with providing more favorable educational opportunities to white students at the expense of their Black and poor peers (*Hobson v. Hansen, 1967*). The union's position at the time was the necessity for the complete racial integration of all District of Columbia staff and students. Even though racial integration for both staff and students is no longer an issue of contention, disparities in the allocation of school resources remain prevalent across the district's eight wards.

Former Union President Davis characterized the achievement gap between racial groups as an opportunity gap emanating from the lack of adequate school funding for the neediest students, due to poverty, housing, and gentrification. In December 2017, the union believed that it had convinced the school district to be part of a meaningful collaboration aimed at addressing the achievement gap issue. The charismatic union president stated when asked about collaboration with the new schools' chancellor,

> One of the very first changes I noticed was that the chancellor saw a need to address school climate and the social side of education. He saw the need to focus more attention on social and emotional

> learning because a high percentage of our students come from communities in which they see and experience a lot of trauma. We have over 3,000 students who are coming to school from homeless shelters in the district, but people do not know that (Ngwa, 2018).

The success of the much-touted collaboration between the WTU and the District of Columbia Public Schools (DCPS) was hamstrung by the sudden forced resignation of the schools' chancellor, Antwan Wilson, a few months into his tenure following a scandal involving school placement for his daughter.

The short tenure of DCPS chancellors, just like the constant teacher churn in the school district, is a source of constant worry for the local union. It critically handicaps much-needed collaboration on programs aligned with the social justice agenda of the WTU. It is worth noting that although the union and the community have longstanding concerns about the social disparities affecting children in the school district, Chancellor Wilson's approach to relations with the union and its members demonstrated his willingness and openness to collaborate. Unfortunately, that was short-lived. Possibly, his immediate successor Amanda Alexander, who served in the interim, would have accepted some of the union's long-held social justice beliefs that could have potentially benefited minority students in the district, but she, too, was replaced within a year.

Alexander, a long-time Washingtonian and career educator for more than 25 years, was not shy about acknowledging the achievement and opportunity gaps that existed in the district. What is unknown is the length at which she was willing to engage with the union in their attempts to address the problem. Under the current chancellor, Lewis Ferebee, DCPS has developed an Equity Framework and clearly pledged to naming institutional bias and persistent disparities in the school district. However, the local union and its allies do not see that as sufficient, especially after an explosive report from a study conducted and published in August 2021 by American University School of Education entitled *Perspectives on D.C.PS IMPACT Evaluation System: Findings from Teachers and School Leaders* (Campbell, et al., 2021) concluded that the teacher evaluation system, IMPACT, was racially biased, especially against women of color.

Community Schools

Although former WTU President Davis knew that some collaboration, such as the community schools' model, was already taking place before the arrival of the new chancellor, more collaboration was needed to expand the number of schools and to improve the 40 lowest-performing schools at the time. What was needed to accomplish turning around the lowest-performing schools was getting the resources and funding to transform those schools into high-performing ones.

Community schools take an integrated approach to learning, using the involvement of all community partners—school, home, health agencies, mental health facilities, the faith-based community, employment agencies, and so forth. They provide the wraparound services that students and families need to thrive. Community schools are not unique to the District of Columbia. The number of existing community schools in the District of Columbia, also called Connected Schools, is less than the number of such schools in other jurisdictions where the teachers' unions have taken an active role in their establishment. The hope is that with more funding, the model will be expanded to benefit students in the most underprivileged parts of the city. Unfortunately, school funding is a very contentious issue in the city, with fewer funds allocated to schools with the greatest need.

Community schools exist and are successful in the cities of Baltimore, Maryland; Austin, Texas; El Paso, Texas; and in many others around the country. The 2019 Maryland Blueprint for Education led to a rapid expansion of community schools and funding (Maryland State Department of Education, 2021. Prince Georges county, the county with the largest Black population in the country, operates 145 community schools (Prince George's County Public Schools, 2025), more than any other city in the country besides New York City. The Prince Georges County Education Association (PGCEA) has long been an advocate of community schools and was instrumental in supporting state legislation (the Blueprint) that expanded funding in 2019 (Prince George's County Educators' Association, n.d.).

Community schools are a true representation of collaboration around school improvement, involving parents, school administrators, teachers, faith-based organizations, and other nonprofits, all to make neighborhood schools a better place for learning. The union backs community schools because they espouse the collaboration that unions have long sought, and because community schools have turned around many struggling schools in the country.

Union support for community schools has not only been a matter of rhetoric, but the AFT has taken concrete action by providing funds to support the operation of community schools. AFT Innovation Grants have benefited jurisdictions in Texas; Daly City, California; Rome, New York; Pittsburgh, Pennsylvania; Peoria, Illinois; Miami, Florida; and San Francisco, California. The Fund awards varying amounts of money depending on availability of funds to local unions that work in collaboration with their school districts to help children and their families to succeed where they would not otherwise thrive (American Federation of Teachers, n.d.). In the words of Randi Weingarten, AFT President: "We're putting skin in the game to incubate and grow education strategies that give kids the supports and options that will help them succeed" (Weingarten, personal communication, January 2025). She underscores that "effective community schooling and career-tech programs do that through powerful engagement and learning, addressing children's well-being beyond academics; strengthening educator capacity; and fostering collaborative efforts among teachers, principals, district officials, families, businesses, nonprofits, and other community groups" (Weingarten, personal communication, January 2025). When a research study published in January 2020 found that New York City community schools reduced chronic absenteeism, improved discipline, and moved students to the next grade, the AFT was the first to react to the positive news, touting its long-held advocacy for community schools. Perhaps even more significant in its advocacy is the support provided to United Teachers Los Angeles in winning one of its demands in the 2019 six-day strike, with that demand being an agreement to transform and the provision of dedicated funding for the conversion of 30 schools into community schools. The most recent collective bargaining agreement between the district and the union included additional funding for community schools.

Overall, the AFT empowered its members to help in the creation of over 700 community schools around the country and continues to work with partners to advocate for the creation of 25,000 community schools by 2025 (Weingarten, 2023).

Local jurisdictions used some of the past Innovation Grants to hire full-time community school coordinators, to develop an Emergency Response Technology academy, to develop computer science programs, and to offer college-entrance-exam preparation, among other programs (American Federation of Teachers, 2017).

In the summer of 2017, the WTU led a delegation of stakeholders to Baltimore City where it visited some successful community schools and has since continued to advocate for an expansion of the model. In the 2018–2019 school year, DCPS introduced what they termed the *Connected Schools Model* and identified ten schools for the initial rollout. The school district has since expanded its offerings to 18 schools under the joint leadership of the schools' administration and Connected Schools managers. According to Latisha Chishlom, former WTU member and former Connected Schools Manager at Anacostia Senior High School, community schools and connected schools just differ in terminology (Chishlom, personal communication, January 2020). Her role as manager involved identifying community needs, identifying assets, and planning where there wasn't a plan. As manager, part of her portfolio, which is characteristic of others working with community schools, was development work—establishing partnerships to provide much needed resources to the schools (DCPS Connected Schools, n.d.).

In my previous role as WTU Executive Director, I had been in quarterly partnership meetings at the district level to help expand community schools, part of which focused on advocating for the funding of the community manager's position through the mayor's office rather than through local school budgets. The approach taken by this local school manager was pretty much in sync with the union's approach to provide paid work-based learning experiences to students, post-secondary transition support, a community-based approach to gun violence, partnerships with local businesses to keep students off the streets, and the expansion of academic and extra-curricular supports to students.

Math Literacy

Between 2017 and 2019, the WTU made one issue the central piece of its social justice initiatives: math literacy for students in the lowest-achievement quartile in the district. Historically, students of color have not fared well in math, which in the long run has disproportionately affected their enrollment in Advanced Placement courses, college admissions, and career success (Washington Teachers' Union, 2021).

Using high-profile civil rights icons such as Dr. Robert (Bob) Moses and the celebrity power of renowned actor Danny Glover, the union organized a first-of-its-kind event at city hall on September 14, 2018, to bring public attention to the disparities that existed in the district around math literacy. The partnership, dubbed the "We the People—Math Literacy for All" alliance, sought to provide resources, support, and an alternative curriculum to targeted students, especially those in one-star low-performing schools, to improve their math literacy skills and to build in students a strong understanding of math (Algebra Project, n.d.) .

After meeting with members of the alliance and partners in other jurisdictions, participating in weekly conference calls, and visiting schools in Boston, Massachusetts, and the Bronx, New York that benefited from Moses's math initiative, the union believed it was time to be more aggressive in engaging the school district to pilot the initiative in some of its schools.

The foundation of this collaboration was laid in the summer of 2017, when then schools' Chancellor Antwan Wilson met with WTU President Davis on the sidelines of Harvard University's Public Education Leadership Project (PELP). A similar meeting took place with interim chancellor Amanda Alexander in the summer of 2018 after Wilson resigned. With Wilson's departure, the goal was to solicit buy-in from Alexander and her team at the District of Columbia Public Schools. Her participation on a panel discussion organized by the union alongside Moses, Glover, and Davis sent a positive signal that the district was making strides in embracing the collaboration, but that too was short-lived following Alexander's replacement in January 2019 with a new chancellor. Although Alexander's replacement, Lewis Ferebee, was open-minded about the attention given to math literacy and acknowledged knowing Moses's work, he was more of a listener at meetings and hardly contributed any ideas to how the collaboration could help the district's struggling Black students. Both the union and its math literacy partners left what was initially a highly anticipated meeting with the chancellor greatly disappointed because he seemed disconnected from the conversation and did not actively participate as they would have loved.

In spite of the lack of collaboration, the WTU forged ahead, sponsoring a team from Turner Elementary School under the leadership of a young teacher, Raphael Bonhomme, to compete at the FLAGWAY tournament organized by the Young People's Project (YPP), an arm of the Algebra Project, in May 2019 under the auspices of the National Math Festival. The YPP touts its success in using FLAGWAY as a means of engaging students in solving prime factorization problems and other math concepts, while at the same time helping them to stay in shape and to compete with their peers (The Young People's Project, n.d.).

In July of the same year, the WTU invited new Chancellor Lewis Ferebee, members of the State Board of Education, and community members to participate in a math conference organized by the National Math Alliance at the University of the District of Columbia. Part of the conference involved a briefing at the Rayburn Congressional Office Building to bring attention to the lack of equity in math literacy, at which the WTU-sponsored FLAGWAY team performed a demonstration of the game. Although DCPS sent a representative, Kim Cherry, to the conference, there was no direct or implied endorsement of the initiative.

Unions' Work With Other Organizations

It is unfair to state that only the unions, especially in the case of the District of Columbia Teachers' Union, care about social justice issues. What is certain, however, is that the unions are more invested and use a megaphone to bring more attention to the issues even where they have not been the initiators.

In the summer of 2017, when the District of Columbia's school leadership, for the first time, invited the union president to the PELP institute, equity was at the center of what they believed was the most urgent issue affecting students in the school district. Later that fall, the school district made equity one of the five priorities under its five-year strategic plan for 2017-2022 (District of Columbia Public Schools, 2017).

The WTU has worked with partner organizations on issues that affect education in general and its members in particular. Prior to the death of Elizabeth Davis in 2021, the union worked with several community-based organizations on social justice initiatives. The faith-based community was very instrumental in fighting against social inequities in the city with Rev. Graylan Hagler, retired minister for the Plymouth Congregational United Church of Christ, constantly taking the lead at WTU organized rallies to advocate for equitable school funding, gun violence prevention in schools, and the hiring of nurses in each school. The D.C. Fiscal Policy Institute was very instrumental in crunching the numbers to expose where there were disparities in school budgets around the city. It is also worth noting that the WTU is a member of the C4DC, a steering committee member for D.C. Jobs with Justice, and a member of the Metropolitan Labor Council, which have all endorsed policies that seek educational equity for the students of the District of Columbia as well as fair treatment of employees and residents of the city. Although these collaborations were not as visible under the previous leadership, including the immediate past president's conspicuous absence on the advisory board of the American University School of Education, the framework for collaboration still exists and simply needs to be exploited to the fullest (American University School of Education, 2025).

At the 2020 Center for School Improvement leadership conference where the focus for 2020 was on culturally responsive pedagogy, the partnership between the AFT and Morningside Center for Teaching Social Responsibility was on full display. Morningside's facilitators engaged participants in difficult conversations around race and confronting racist practices in schools using *restorative circles* (Morningside Center for Teaching Social Responsibility, 2020). For the AFT, confronting institutional injustices requires a communal approach, and so, bringing in other organizations to help teachers, school administrators, and community members to combat racist tendencies in schools is not unusual. AFT's president has not shied away from directly confronting social injustices around the country, regardless of the jurisdiction.

Institutional Bias

DCPS's acknowledgment of the existence of institutional bias against students of color and disparities in the allocation of school resources was a welcome move for the union, but not enough to solve the problem. Additionally, the focus on social-emotional learning as a means of educating the whole child was laudable, but from the union's point of view, poorly rolled out. Since then, the union has continued to be vocal about the lack of transparency around school funding and the continuous disparity across the eight wards of the district.

The union also brought in outside equity consultants to provide training to its members with the goal of better serving students. Both DCPS and the WTU agree on culturally responsive pedagogy, alternatives to punitive disciplinary actions that disproportionately affect students of color, social-emotional learning, and trauma-informed teaching (tailoring instruction to meet the needs of students who have undergone traumatic situations). DCPS has developed an Equity Framework and is actively working to dismantle institutional bias against all student demographics. However, such efforts appeared to be undercut by an American University study report that revealed that the teacher evaluation system is biased against teachers of color. There has always been an outcry over racial bias against Black women in the district's teacher evaluation system since it was instituted by Michelle Rhee, but no structured study like the one from American University has ever before made that determination in its findings (Campbell et al., 2021).

The union uses the annual Shared Vision Conference to showcase its collaboration and generally engages other stakeholders to facilitate workshops. In the past, the school district has offered sessions on social-emotional learning and trauma-informed teaching, while selected union rank-and-file members, parents, and outside consultants have facilitated sessions on family engagement, school budgets, culturally informed teaching, and equity in schools, among other topics (Washington Teachers' Union, 2025).

Championing the Needs of Students

Teachers and their unions champion the needs of students, and the community stands with them. During teachers' union protests and strikes in 2018 and 2019 in West Virginia, Oklahoma, Arizona, Denver, Los Angeles, and Oakland, teachers did not focus solely on traditional union bread-and-butter issues. Even though they demanded better wages commensurate with the standard of living in their respective localities, they fundamentally made a case for smaller class sizes as a bedrock for effective teaching. They demanded more funding and resources for their students. Before engaging in a work stoppage action, union members in West Virginia made plans to take care of their most vulnerable students, working with school board members to pack lunches for needy students who normally received assistance through the McDowell County *Blessings in a Backpack* program. That is the caring attitude that labor unions exude, and to characterize them as obstructionists or protectionist of bad employees is a mischaracterization too often foisted by conservative anti-union groups and school choice proponents.

In Chicago, the Chicago Teachers' Union and the city failed to make progress in their 2019 contract negotiations because the city failed to enact the union's "preferred affordable housing policy as part of their contract," (Shropshire, 2019, p. 1) according to the mayor. Even though the city deemed the issue a non-bargaining issue, the union argued that "we have nearly 17,000 homeless students in CPS" on whose behalf they were advocating. They contended that part of their proposal demanded that more support staff be hired to help families in danger of losing housing, and noted that advocating for affordable housing was a necessity. Although the mayor did not deem the bargaining table as the most appropriate venue for such a conversation, the union believed that the collective bargaining process was where they had the most leverage to address the issue. Consequently, the strike dragged on for 11 days, with the union demanding more nurses, social workers, and librarians and smaller class sizes to better serve their students. Championing the needs of students has prevailed in both liberal and conservative states, a phenomenon that has become known as bargaining for the common good.

In the February 2023 mayoral elections in Chicago, the teachers' union took its activism in support of social justice a step further, propelling former teacher and union member Brandon Johnson to the finish line as mayor. The union's alliances with progressive allies and its social justice agenda helped elect the candidate they deemed audacious enough to shake up the status quo and steward its vision for students, educators, and the community at large (Lazare, 2024). *The Nation Magazine* characterizes the Chicago Teachers' Union as "the boldest local union in America" that "has assembled a broad coalition of community groups, progressive unions, and leftist elected officials around a shared agenda of fighting the austerity, poverty, racism, and gentrification that have reshaped Chicago politics in the past decade and a half." The CTU is known for its militantism to advocate for working class people in the city and for standing up vociferously for its communities.

Public School Funding

Teachers' unions are relentless in their efforts to advocate for increased and proportionate public-school funding. In 2018, the AFT published a report *A Decade of Neglect: Public Education Funding in the Aftermath of the Great Recession* to underscore, among other budgetary issues, that underfunding of K–12 education has occurred in every single state in the United States of America after the Great Recession. The report further identified 25 states, which as of 2016, were still providing less funding for K–12 education than they did before the Recession, counting inflation (American Federation of Teachers, 2018). The report revealed that:

- Schools in these states have been shortchanged by $19 billion.
- Eighteen of the 25 states that provided less funding for K–12 education reduced their tax effort between 2008 and 2015.

- The ten worst states for per-pupil funding in 2016 either reduced their overall tax effort or took action that had a net negative impact on revenue after 2008.
- In 35 states, between 2008 and 2016, the ratio of students to teachers grew (American Federation of Teachers, 2018, p. 4).

Public Funds for Private and Charter Schools

Unions regard the funding of private and public charter schools using public money as a diversion of critical funds that could be used to improve conventional or traditional public schools. Education researchers have long taken the side of unions that charter schools and school vouchers pose fundamental challenges to America's existing K–12 public educational system. Even though private and charter schools receive public funding, local governments do not hold them to the same accountability standards as neighborhood traditional public schools. Diane Ravitch has written extensively about the effects of charter school funding and school choice on traditional public schools (Ravitch, 2025).

Unions' advocacy for school funding is a recurring event through their Fund Our Future and Red for Ed campaigns to bring public attention to inadequate and unsustainable funding for public schools, colleges, and universities. The Fund Our Future campaign, the National Education Association's Red for Ed, and other initiatives spearheaded by these organizations and their locals remind legislators and the public of their civic duties to educate the leaders of tomorrow. These campaigns urge legislators to fulfill that promise of educating our future leaders through adequate public school funding (American Federation of Teachers, n.d.; National Education Association, n.d.).

The advocacy issue is an attempt to remind those in power that they cannot continue to slash public school budgets. Ruthlessly cutting school budgets is an assault on children. It weakens our democracy. The assault will continue without strong advocates in state houses and on Capitol Hill. The adults who teach and nurture the children and youth daily in dilapidated classrooms using outdated books are taking the lead to stand up to defend their students through advocacy.

The amount of money spent on standardized testing has deprived public schools of money that could fund critical programs that are instrumental in the education of the whole child. The obsession with standardized testing cannot be a substitute for current textbooks; reasonable class sizes; healthy lunches; the inclusion of art, music, foreign languages, libraries, and counseling services; modern technology; school nurses; and social-emotional programs.

Charter school and school choice opponents strongly believe that the proliferation of charter schools and school choice has added to the growing fiscal pains that public schools endure. AFT and its allies share this school of thought, especially in cities with a high number of charter schools. There is no denying that the American public education system has deficiencies and needs serious reforms, but the reforms cannot come through the fiscal deprivation of government-operated local education agencies or the elimination of the Department of Education that provides critical funding and supports to public schools.

Scapegoating Teachers and Their Unions

Despites teachers' and their unions' efforts to protect the interests of public schools around the country, the unions have been scapegoated and accused of obstructing improvement and accountability measures. Reforming the American education system entails a bottom-up approach, which is what unions have advocated for, for a long time. Top-down measures of accountability through the federal No Child Left Behind and Race to the Top legislation have not succeeded in reforming the system. Moreover, using standardized testing and punitive merit-based measures of teacher evaluation are counterproductive examples, which abound in cities such as Washington, D.C.

Lack of Progress in Student Achievement

According to an analysis by The Center for Media and Democracy's PR Watch, between 2019 and 2014, testing companies Pearson Education, Educational Testing Service, McGraw-Hill, and Houghton

Mifflin collectively spent more than 20 million dollars lobbying lawmakers in Congress and in local State Houses (The Center for Media and Democracy, 2015). The amount of money spent on charter schools, which are held to different accountability standards, has worsened an already-bad situation because the data to substantiate any real progress in student achievement is either sparse or nonexistent.

Charter Schools

The Partnership for Assessment of Readiness for College and Careers (PARCC) is an annual assessment based on the Common Core State Standards and used by a consortium of states, including the District of Columbia, to measure students' proficiency in Mathematics and Reading (District of Columbia Public Schools, 2025).

After the release of the 2019 PARCC results by the D.C. Office of the State Superintendent of Education, the fact that charter schools failed to perform at a level comparable to their peers in the traditional public-school setting prompted public outrage. Ironically, Scott Pearson, the executive director of the D.C. Public Charter School Board, in reaction, stated that he had encouraged the board to emulate some of the growth strategies used by the traditional public-school sector in English Language Learning (Lerner, 2019).

Increasingly, the public is becoming critical of charter schools for siphoning both funds and students from traditional public schools in what some critics have characterized as a failed experiment. Some are calling for a moratorium on the opening of new charter schools.

For a good number of years, attempts at unionizing charter schools have failed. It is no coincidence that charter school operators have fought strenuously to disrupt any union activities on their campuses. Charter schools have the latitude to hire and fire teachers at will because they are exempt from some of the bureaucratic regulations such as collective bargaining that are imposed on traditional public schools. Unionizing charter schools would mean that their educators would have the right to bargain collectively for their compensation and benefits. Resistance to collective bargaining and other non-accountability measures has prompted unions to accuse charter schools' operators of a culture of oppression and of using public money to enrich themselves, by spending less on their teachers and students.

When the WTU ratified its Collective Bargaining Agreement with DCPS in 2016, charter schools in the city benefited from a comparable 9 percent raise that their members were entitled to for the next three years, thanks to federal law that requires equal funding for operational costs in both local education agencies (DC Fiscal Policy Institute, 2024). Similarly, in the most recently ratified contract in 2023 between the two bargaining agents, charter schools were again expected to receive a proportionate percentage of salary increases (Collins, 2023). Unfortunately, in the 2016 contract, charter school teachers did not necessarily benefit from the pay increases. However, charter school administrators earned some of the highest salaries in the city, ranging between $171,000 and $541,000 per year. In February 2023, the leaders of D.C.'s charter school network pledged in a letter to the mayor and deputy mayor for education that the pay increases emanating from the ratified WTU-DCPS contract would be dedicated exclusively to their teachers' pay raises. Unfair practices like the one cited here further erode the unions' and the public's trust in charter schools.

Even though the city funds charter schools publicly, individual schools are exempt from the Freedom of Information Act (Board of Ethics and Government Accountability, n.d.). This issue became the subject of 2019 city council hearings with the WTU, parents, and other community allies requesting greater transparency from charter operators. The D.C. public continues to request greater transparency around this issue, arguing that individual charter schools are considered local education agencies and should be held to the same standards as D.C. public schools. While the salaries of all District of Columbia government employees, including DCPS teachers, are public information, the DC Public Charter School Board only started sharing this information starting in SY 2025-2026 (DC Public Charter School Board, 2025). The lack of accountability and transparency has enabled charter operators to fire teachers at will and send disruptive students to unlicensed residences that have no affiliation with the educational, social, and emotional well-being of children.

In December 2018, for example, the *Washington Post* reported that the city was investigating an unlicensed learning center that served as a temporary warehouse for disruptive students before they were eventually transferred to other schools. One of the charter schools whose students were sent to the facility admitted that the school determined it was unable to meet the students' special education needs and sent them to be held at the center to await a transfer to an appropriate setting (Stein & Strauss, 2018).

Compromising the safety of children is something that unions care deeply about and will continue to fight against as long as students are in danger. The privately-operated charter schools are resistant to their teachers organizing because those teachers will do just what their counterparts around the country do every single day—stand up for their students. It is no surprise then that Cesar Chavez Public Charter School, the only charter school in their city that successfully unionized, announced in January 2019 that it would be closing its doors (District of Columbia Public Charter School Board, 2019). Chavez would not be the first charter in the city to close, but unlike the previous charter school, Excel Academy, which closed at the end of the 2017–2018 academic year due to low student performance, the speculation, in this case, was that the closure was to thwart union influence and the accountability that it brings. However, DCPS took over the school and assigned one of its high-performing principals and 2018 principal of the year, Tenia Pritchard, to lead it (O'Gorek, 2018).

To demonstrate how much money is siphoned from public schools to benefit charter schools, Excel Academy leased its premises from the D.C. government. However, upon its closure, it still held an active, long-term lease with the city and, in turn, rented the facility out to the latter to operate its public school (Stein, 2019) .

AFT and NEA Both Stand Against Social Injustices

There may be philosophical differences between the way the AFT and NEA operate, with the latter historically identifying as a professional organization, but when it comes to contemporary issues, both are united in taking a common stance against social injustices. The NEA has also been a loud voice for the weak and helpless on issues regarding college affordability and the burden of student loan debt on its members, taking the lead on human and civil rights issues, gun violence, disasters, immigration, the rights of LGBTQ students, and a wide range of other issues that the public cares about passionately (National Education Association, n.d.; American Federation of Teachers, n.d.).

On a cold winter evening in February 2017, I was privileged to host a rally at Upper Senate Park across the street from the U.S. Capitol to urge senators not to vote for the confirmation of Betsy DeVos as President Donald Trump's Education Secretary. Two of the high-profile personalities that I introduced were the charismatic presidents of the NEA and AFT, Lily Eskelsen García and Randi Weingarten respectively. When I stood on that podium and introduced Lily, Randi, and other leaders, at no point did it cross my mind that they belonged to separate organizations and represented the interests of different constituencies.

All I saw and heard were passionate leaders who cared about the young citizens of the United States and were committed to protecting their futures. What I am also certain about is that they cared less about what my organizational affiliation was, but rather banded with my colleagues and me to oppose the confirmation of someone whose background and actions promised a very bleak future for our children. That is what unions do. They show up; they stand up against what is wrong; they speak for the voiceless; and they give hope to the hopeless. Unfortunately, the Republican majority in the Senate went on to confirm Betsy DeVos as Education Secretary.

Opposition to DeVos

When unions opposed the confirmation of Betsy DeVos, they based their opposition on fears that she would do what she did over her four years' tenure. She cut federal funding for public education; eliminated protections for vulnerable groups of students such as LGBTQ students, immigrant students, and non-English language learners;

and she protected the financial industry that is responsible for the financial plight of many college graduates.

Worse still was the amount of money that she allocated to school vouchers. Her introduction of the Education Freedom Scholarships and Opportunity Act in February 2019 was further evidence that she was bent on starving public schools of funding and creating opportunities that benefited her friends. This act allocated up to $5 billion annually toward school choice with no simultaneous increase in public education allocations (Education Freedom Scholarships and Opportunity Act, 2019). Actions like this deprive most students in the United States who attend traditional public schools (National Center for Education Statistics, 2024) yet face annual budget shortfalls for critical programs such as special education, arts, music, and world languages.

The opposition against Betsy DeVos was not only from unions, but it was also from parents, students, the faith-based community, and the hardworking men and women who care about the education and welfare of their children and have continued to partner with unions.

Vouchers and Students With Disabilities

Beneficiaries of school vouchers exclude students who have special needs. These students return to the public education system, which ends up as the sole system with the resources to meet their needs. Unfortunately, parents are not aware of the limits of the school voucher program. The Individuals with Disabilities Education Act (IDEA) guarantees a free and appropriate public education (FAPE) which covers students with disabilities. A major provision of the law is that these students will be taught in the least-restrictive environment, which directly implies that they will have access to general education classes with their peers. These protections that are afforded families by law do not follow them to the private educational environment when the parent or caregiver decides to benefit from the school voucher system (USDOE, n.d.).

Because there is no accountability for private schools that benefit from public dollars, most often the private schools do not and are not obligated to afford students with special needs the accommodations guaranteed in IDEA. A report published by the Government Accountability Office (GAO) in November 2017 estimated that no more than half of participating schools in any voucher program mentioned students with disabilities on their websites (U.S. Government Accountability Office, 2017). These schools did not notify parents of students with disabilities of the changes in their rights when they moved their children from the public-school space to private schools. Although the GAO recommended that Congress require states to tell parents and guardians of the changes to federal special education rights when students transition from public to private school, that recommendation is still in limbo.

Asking for accountability from entities that receive public money and seeking protections for the most vulnerable is not a matter of more wages or benefits for union members. What is evident is that because of financial contributions made to the Republican party, the charter schools and religiously affiliated schools receive extra benefits taken from public school budgets. However, too often, public officials on the Right cannot muster the courage to stand up and hold non-public schools accountable.

Student-Loan Debt

An exacerbation of the plight of the public-school system occurs with the growing pains numerous teachers experience in response to their student-loan debt. The AFT's survey on the effects of student debt on its members found that student debt was the major driver of financial difficulties leading to other effects such as the inability to save for retirement, psychological problems, lack of home ownership, poor credit ratings, and the inability to provide for children's needs (American Federation of Teachers, 2018). Testifying before the U.S. House of Representatives' House Ways and Means Committee in February 2019, Tatum Tirado, mathematics teacher at D.C.'s Ballou High School and member of the Washington Teachers' Union, had this to say:

> I have a huge amount of student debt from graduate school. I am living on a single teacher's income with a very expensive health

> condition, and two gifted children (their schools have officially classified them both as gifted; these are not just the words of a proud mother). I would love to supplement their educations with enrichment or extracurricular activities such as piano or violin lessons, but I cannot afford to (Tirado, 2019).

Over the years, the AFT has worked with Tatum and other members to testify before the Senate Banking Subcommittee on Financial Institutions and Consumer Protection (www.banking.senate.gov) on the effects of high student loan interest rates and debt, as well as before the House Ways and Means Committee on the devastating effects of student loans on their career advancement. Not only has the AFT brought public attention to and sought legislative action on the issue, but the union is constantly taking action to avert the further damage to victims of corporate greed in the form of high-interest loans.

Consequently, the AFT has provided resources to manage and reduce payments, organized regular student debt clinics to help members apply for student loan forgiveness, and provided financial wellness resources to help individuals increase their credit scores and manage household expenses. The union's member survey uncovered several other issues that do not apply to everyone at the same level. Student loan debt disproportionately affects members along racial and age lines, with African Americans and younger borrowers hit the hardest (American Federation of Teachers, 2018).

In terms of loan servicers, the survey identified Navient as the highest servicer of student loans. A 2018 class-action lawsuit filed by nine AFT members in four states against Navient accused them of misleading and stopping borrowers who are public employees from applying for the ten-year Public Service Loan Forgiveness program to boost its profits (American Federation of Teachers, 2018).

In July of 2019, the AFT filed a class lawsuit against the U.S. Department of Education for deliberately blocking borrowers' access to the Public Service Loan Forgiveness program. The Biden administration immediately moved to settle that lawsuit, paving the way for millions of borrowers to benefit from the loan forgiveness program. Actions such as this demonstrate the extent to which the organization advocates, not only for its members but for the public in general in terms of correcting social injustices.

Student-debt clinics became very popular among union members because of the assistance that the loan servicers were intentionally not providing to borrowers. During the approximately 90-minute sessions, unions provided resources to their members who struggled with monthly payments on student loans to benefit from the Public Service Loan Forgiveness program. Information provided during the sessions included counseling on how to enroll in income-driven repayment plans and how to use the power of the union to be more active in their advocacy for social justice and other issues.

In response to Education Secretary Betsy DeVos's rewrite of the Borrower Defense Rule in 2018, AFT President Randi Weingarten wrote:

> With great fanfare, Betsy DeVos and the Education Department have announced changes to the borrower defense rule that President Obama's administration enacted to stop for-profit colleges and loan servicers from ripping off students.
>
> The good news is, because of the advocacy of students and young adults saddled with college debt, as well as the AFT and other allies, they wouldn't dare end the rule. The bad news is that what has been proposed is far different than DeVos' spin.
>
> Her rewrite makes it harder for defrauded students to get the relief they need and easier for predatory for-profits to get away with ripping off students. It presumes a student is guilty, and the profit-driven institutions are innocent by raising the evidence standard for students. It could make borrowers wait until they default before they can apply to have their loan discharged. It makes it harder for students to get relief from closed schools or for groups of students to get relief, as happened with defrauded Corinthian Colleges students. And it ends the ban on mandatory arbitration. Further, the department's position that federal actions pre-empt state statutes is intended to limit state lawmakers and their attorneys general from protecting borrowers. It appears this is a rule written by the for-profit college industry to support the for-profit college industry.

> Predatory practices by certain so-called colleges across the country have financially gutted working people—many of them first-generation college students, veterans and people of color—while offering them the false hope of a good job and a fair wage. Just about the only thing worse than ripping off students with worthless degrees from for-profit colleges is denying them help to relieve their substantial debt and allowing the schools to continue to prey on students. Once again, DeVos has abandoned her responsibility to students to prop up an industry littered with fraud and bad actors (American Federation of Teachers, 2020).

The aggressive advocacy of the union opened the doors for millions of union members to benefit from the Public Service Loan Forgiveness Program under the Biden administration.

School Improvement

The AFT believes in collaborating with all stakeholders to improve educational outcomes for students and uses the annual Center for School Improvement (CSI) as an avenue to bring together school districts and local school teams. During an electrifying address at the 2019 CSI at the United Federation of Teachers' headquarters in New York, AFT President Randi Weingarten underscored the issues that all education stakeholders cared about, prompting a standing ovation from the attending school and district administrators, teachers, and community advocates.

"Teachers wake up every day wanting to help students; no teacher wakes up saying 'I want to make a student's life worse'," (Weingarten, 2019, personal communication) screamed Randi to thunderous applause from the audience. No other speaker could have framed the issues that unions care about more than she did, citing and underscoring the numerous advocacy programs that unions undertake on behalf of students, but which union opponents selectively ignore in their rhetoric.

She described, among other things, programs intended to empower young people otherwise referred to as *youth voices*. At every CSI that I have attended, young people have narrated emotional and compelling stories of their advocacy and strength in the face of adversity, most of which have been supported and sponsored by the AFT. While others have shared stories of rejection due to their sexual orientation and how much advocacy has propelled them to the level of acceptance within their communities, others have narrated stories of standing up against gun violence in their communities in Chicago, Illinois and Parkland, Florida.

Partnerships With Other Groups

Union advocacy for social justice has garnered partnerships within and beyond the borders of the United States. Whether it is rebuilding in the aftermath of Hurricane Maria in Puerto Rico or supporting the Hand in Hand education coalition in Israel, the AFT is standing up for what is right. The AFT and its locals also support other organizations and causes that align with their goals, among them the Alliance to Reclaim Our Schools which supports educational justice and equity, First Book which helps bring free and low-cost books to underprivileged communities, the Food Research and Action Center that promotes healthy nutrition policies, the Special Olympics, and others. Local unions are building coalitions with other labor unions to band together on issues of interest in their communities. Within the Washington metropolitan area, District of Columbia Jobs with Justice (DCJWJ) and Teaching for Change have closely collaborated with the WTU to fight for social justice causes. The Metropolitan Labor Council's Evening with Labor in 2019 publicly acknowledged the DCJWJ for standing closely with the nurses at Providence Hospital to protest the closure of the hospital. In the past, together with the nurses' union and the WTU, they supported petitions to the D.C. City Council, advocating for full-time nurses at each D.C. public school (Harris, 2018). Teaching for Change has developed a full curriculum and provides training to members of the WTU on culturally informed teaching. In 2017, Teaching for Change recognized the WTU president, Elizabeth Davis, for her aggressive role in standing up for District of Columbia students.

Teachers' unions are not sitting back and complaining or waiting for someone else to improve on the quality of their teaching or on closing the achievement gap. They are proposing solutions.

Further Reading

Algebra Project. (n.d.). Math Literacy for All. https://mathliteracyforall.org/values

American Federation of Teachers. (2017). *Collaborating to Expand CTE Offerings: The Pittsburgh Federation of Teachers, local 400* (Report). https://www.aft.org/sites/default/files/media/2017/if_pft-cte_2017.pdf

American Federation of Teachers. (2018a). *A decade of neglect: Public education funding in the aftermath of the Great Recession.* https://www.aft.org/decade-neglect

American Federation of Teachers. (2018b). *Class-action lawsuit launched against student loan servicer Navient over PSLF.* https://www.aft.org/press-release/class-action-lawsuit-launched-against-student-loan-servicer-navient-over

American Federation of Teachers. (2018c). *2018 AFT student debt survey.* https://www.aft.org/sites/default/files/media/2018/studentdebtsurvey.pdf

American Federation of Teachers. (2020). *AFT President Randi Weingarten responds to DeVos "borrower defense" rule rewrite.* https://www.aft.org/news/house-slaps-down-devos-policy-student-debt

American Federation of Teachers. (n.d.). *Our community.* https://www.aft.org/our-community/

American University School of Education. (2025). *Board members, SOE.* https://www.american.edu/soe/board.cfm

Anderson, J (2017). *Charter Schools Are Getting a Free Ride off of Unionized Public School Teachers.* Washington City Paper.

Board of Ethics and Government Accountability. (n.d.). *FOIA advisory opinions.* Open DC. https://www.open-dc.gov/documents/foia-advisory-opinions

Brown v. Board of Educ., 347 U.S. 483 (1954).

Campbell C.M., Parker, C., Shand,R., Kelly-Massoud, A., Fashola, T., and Blanc, J. (2021): Perspectives on DCPS IMPACT Teacher Evaluation System: Findings from Teachers and School Leaders. American University School of Education.

The Center for Media and Democracy. (2015). Pearson, ETS, Houghton Mifflin, and McGraw-Hill lobby big and profit bigger from school tests: A CMD reporters' guide. Madison, WI: J. Persson. http://www. prwatch.org

Civic Impulse. (2017a). H.R. 1 — 107th Congress: No Child Left Behind Act of 2001. https://www.govtrack.us/congress/bills/107/hr1

Civic Impulse. (2017b). H.R. 1532 — 112th Congress: Race to the Top Act of 2001. https://www.govtrack.us/congress/bills/112/hr1

Collective Bargaining Agreement, Washington Teachers' Union-District of Columbia Public Schools, 1968–1969.

Collins, S. P.K. (2023). *Matching Teachers' Funds Raises Questions of Public Charter School Unions.* Washington: The Informer.

DC Fiscal Policy Institute. (2024). *How DC funds its public schools.* https://www.dcfpi.org/all/how-dc-funds-its-public-schools/

DCPS Connected Schools. (n.d.). *Our model.* https://www.dcpsconnectedschools.org/our-model

District of Columbia Public Schools. (2017). *A Capital Commitment: Strategic Plan 2017-2022.* https://dcps.dc.gov/publication/dcps-strategic-plan-capital-commitment-2017-2022

District of Columbia Public Schools. (2025). *DCPS data set - PARCC.* https://dcps.dc.gov/publication/dcps-data-set-parcc

DC Public Charter School Board. (2025). *Transparency Hub.* https://dcpcsb.org/transparency-hub

District of Columbia Public Charter School Board. (2019). *Campus closure and consolidation - Cesar Chavez PCS.* DC PCSB. https://www.dcpcsb.org/campus-closure-and-consolidation-cesar-chavez-pcs-0

Education Freedom Scholarships and Opportunity Act, S. 634, 116th Cong. (2019). Congress.gov. https://www.congress.gov/bill/116th-congress/senate-bill/634/text

Good, R. M. (2025). Charterization, Gentrification, and the Geography of Opening and Closing Schools in Washington, D.C. *Education and Urban Society, 57*(1), 40–62. https://doi.org/10.1177/00131245241265098

Harris, N. (2018). *Planned closure of Providence Hospital services draws protests.* The DC Line. https://thedcline.org/2018/09/25/planned-closure-of-providence-hospital-services-draws-protests/

Hobson v. Hansen, 269 F. Supp. 401 (D.D.C. 1967).

Individuals With Disabilities Education Act, 20 U.S.C., § 1400, and (2004).

Lazare, S. (2024). *The Chicago Teachers Union wants to end student homelessness at the bargaining table.* The Nation. https://www.thenation.com/article/activism/chicago-teachers-union-homelessness/

Lerner, M. (2019). *The D.C. charter school experiment is over.* Parents Have School Choice Kids Win. https://parentshaveschoolchoicekidswin.com/2019/08/20/the-d-c-charter-school-experiment-is-over/

Maier, A., Daniel J., & Oakes J. (2017). *Community Schools as an Effective School Improvement Strategy.* Learning Policy Institute.

Maryland State Department of Education. (2021). *Community schools + concentration of poverty grants.* Blueprint for Maryland's Future. https://blueprint.marylandpublicschools.org/community-schools

Meyersohn, N. (2019). *Walmart ends all handgun ammunition sales and asks customers not to carry guns into stores.* CNN Business. https://www.cnn.com/2019/09/03/business/walmart-ends-handgun-ammo-sales

Morningside Center for Teaching Social Responsibility. (2020). *Restorative circles.* https://www.morningsidecenter.org/restorative-circles

National Center for Education Statistics. (2024). *Back-to-school statistics.* U.S. Department of Education. https://nces.ed.gov/fastfacts/display.asp?id=372.

National Education Association. (n.d.). *Our issues.* https://www.nea.org/advocating-for-change/action-center/our-issues

Ngwa, T. C. (2018). "Fostering Organizational Change Through a Solutions-Driven Culture of Collaboration: A Case Study of a Teachers' Union in the Mid-Atlantic Region." College of Education.

Nowicki, J. M. (2017). *Private School Choice: Federal Actions Needed to Ensure Parents Are Notified About Changes in Rights for Students with Disabilities* (GAO-18-94). U.S. Government Accountability Office.

O'Gorek, E. (2018). *Change comes to Excel Academy. East of the River DC News.* https://eastoftheriverdcnews.com/2018/04/16/change-comes-to-excel-academy/

Prince George's County Educators' Association. (n.d.). *Community schools.* Prince George's County Educators' Association. https://pgcea.org/community-schools/

Prince George's County Public Schools. (2025). *Schools designated as community schools.* https://www.pgcps.org/offices/community-schools/schools-designated-as-community-schools

Ravitch, D. (2025). *Charter Schools* [Education Blog]. Diane Ravitch's Blog. https://dianeravitch.net/category/charter-schools/

Reeve, R. (2018). D.C. high school students gather for gun violence summit. WJLA News. https://wjla.com/news/local/students-gather-for-gun-violence-summit

Shropshire, C. (2019). *CPS teachers want an affordable housing provision in their contract: It's among the new topics starting to land on bargaining tables. Chicago Tribune.* https://www.chicagotribune.com/2019/10/09/cps-teachers-want-an-affordable-housing-provision-in-their-contract-its-among-the-new-topics-starting-to-land-on-bargaining-tables/

Stein, P. & Strauss, V. (2018). *D.C. officials investigate facility where charter schools send disruptive students.* Washington Post.

Stein, P. (2019). *This building shows how complicated school real estate can be in D.C.* The Washington Post. https://www.washingtonpost.com/local/education/this-building-shows-how-complicated-school-real-estate-can-be-in-dc/2019/12/15/78eaf10a-1c70-11ea-8d58-5ac3600967a1_story.htm

The Young People's Project. (n.d.). *The Young People's Project.* https://www.typp.org/.

Thich Nhat Hanh. (1992). Peace is every step: The path of mindfulness in everyday life [Trade paperback ed.]. Bantam Books.

Tirado, T. (2019, March). *[Testimony submitted to the House Ways and Means Committee].* Ways and Means Committee, U.S. House of Representatives. https://waysandmeans.house.gov/wp-content/uploads/2019/03/Tatum-Tirado-testimony.pdf

U.S. Department of Education, Office of Non-Public Education & Office of Special Education Programs. (n.d.). *IDEA: Children with disabilities enrolled by their parents in private schools.* https://www.ed.gov/sites/ed/files/about/inits/ed/non-public-education/files/idea-parentally.pdf

U.S. Government Accountability Office. (2017). *Private school choice: Federal actions needed to ensure parents are notified about changes in rights for students with disabilities* (GAO-18-94). https://www.gao.gov/products/gao-18-94

Washington Teachers' Union. (2021). *Shared forms.* WTU Local 6. https://www.wtulocal6.net/forms/shares/new?page_id=416

Washington Teachers' Union. (2025). *Shared Vision Conference.* WTU Local 6. https://www.wtulocal6.net/shared_vision_conference

Weingarten, R. (2023. *Real solutions for kids and communities.* American Federation of Teachers. https://www.aft.org/column/real-solutions-kids-and-communities

Wolf, P.J., Witt, J.F., & Kisida, B. (2018). *Do Voucher Students Attain Higher Levels of Education?* Urban Institute: 1–16.

CHAPTER 2

Developing Effective Teachers

We are what we repeatedly do. Excellence, then is not an act but a habit.

— Aristotle

The need for career growth and advancement is one that motivates professionals in all fields. As this need has grown, employers have intentionally established mentoring and coaching programs and designed professional development (PD), retention, and accountability measures to help their employees perform at high levels. Teachers, along with other professionals in their respective fields, acknowledge this need for professional growth and accountability. They support PD that enables them to improve their day-to-day practice, which eventually leads to career advancement. It is unconscionable to think that any teacher gets into the profession with the intention of remaining stagnant or of opposing oversight by supervisors.

What remains a source of concern is top-down PD that does not address the immediate needs of the professional in the classroom, punitive evaluation systems, merit pay, and value-added measures of teacher evaluation. Teachers in particular have generally decried PD offerings that do not take their input into consideration, are not informed by data, and consequently don't meet their needs or the needs of their students. It is therefore not uncommon for teachers to use school district PD time for grading or recordkeeping or, in some cases, playing with their handheld devices during sessions due to boredom. What tends to matter during these mandated times is attendance rather than the full impact of the PD offerings. In response, teachers' unions have developed their own PD offerings and sought collaboration with school districts to ensure that their members are acquiring the necessary skills to be successful in the classroom. The focus on developing effective teachers has garnered much support for the union at a time when maintaining membership is not compulsory. Building collaborative partnerships with management, corporations, and the community at large to help teachers improve on their students' outcomes has become the norm. Rather than sitting on the sidelines and agonizing, unions have organized and provided solutions to developing the job effectiveness of their members.

Teacher Quality—Professional Development and Support

The major teachers' unions and their locals have prioritized professional support for their members in addition to continuously advocating for job protections which have traditionally constituted the foundation of organized labor. The AFT in particular offers a wide array of year-round research-informed professional development options to its members. These range from general to specialized content-based offerings, as well as collaborative opportunities geared toward improving teaching and learning.

AFT's *Share My Lesson* platform has become an incredibly resource-filled repository for the over 1.8 million members of the union. The website is designed for anyone who works with students in PreK–12 to exchange curricular ideas and share best practices in the profession (American Federation of Teachers, n.d.). Through partnerships with Discovery Education, Google Applied Digital Skills, Folger Shakespeare Library, and many others, teachers in different content areas and grade levels are able to access lesson plans, professional development webinars, handouts, assessments, and other activities. It is one of the numerous ways, in addition to targeted professional development offerings, that not only members but also parents can obtain resources to support students. Teachers at all levels join the union as a professional organization that is invested in supporting them to be effective, and having access to a platform of this nature makes them want to belong even more. The yearning for ongoing professional learning has increased the demand for and rates of attendance at AFT-organized conferences, the most popular being the annual Teach Conference.

Teacher quality is intended to develop the best teachers in each classroom and to hold them accountable; it remains a top priority of teachers' unions. Several joint initiatives exist between several districts and unions to revamp teacher and principal evaluations including those in the ABC Unified School District, California; Hillsborough County, Florida, Public Schools; Norfolk School District, Virginia; Plattsburgh City Public School District, New York; St. Francis Independent School District, Minnesota; Montgomery County Public Schools, Maryland; and Toledo City School District, among others.

The AFT and the NEA see collaboration around teacher quality, in particular, as a way to *"move in the same direction, and the direction is about kids, the education of students, creating the right environment to educate students"* (Sawchuk & Heitin, 2014, p. 12). Although there is no clear-cut uniformity on how to go about making improvements to teacher quality, there is general agreement, at least within union ranks, that teachers need support in the classroom to better serve their students and families.

Teacher Evaluation

Teacher evaluation remains a very contentious issue and a source of anxiety among union members. In response, union leadership has explored ways to seek protections for their members through collaboration with school districts. Peer Assistance Review (PAR) exists in some districts as a joint effort between management and labor to support and hold teachers accountable. Under PAR, teachers take ownership of the quality of teaching through collaboration with administrators to support and evaluate teachers. Under this evaluation tool, when an administrator determines that a teacher is marginal in their performance, a consulting teacher, who is a member of the teachers' union, conducts a separate observation to make their determination. If the consulting teacher makes the same determination of the teacher's ineffectiveness, only then would the teacher move to the next step of the process, which is providing adequate support to the teacher through coaching and other mechanisms to become successful.

The U.S. Department of Education's Race to the Top (RTTT) initiative under the Obama administration encouraged collaboration between school districts and unions on teacher evaluation. RTTT and other federal policies incentivized states to revamp their teacher evaluation systems, typically tying pay to high teacher-performance ratings or student outcomes. Changes made to teacher evaluation systems resulted in losses to teachers' unions, notably the removal of tenure from collective bargaining agreements, dismissals resulting from the inability to be highly rated due to low student test scores, and unannounced observations (District of Columbia Public Schools, n.d.).

Joint Responsibility

Several joint initiatives by districts and unions to revamp their teacher and principal evaluation systems inspired President Obama's education secretary, Arne Duncan, to travel to Hillsborough County, Florida, on October 14, 2010, in the company of AFT and NEA presidents to announce a labor-management conference. The U.S. Department of Education (USDOE) labor-management conference in 2011 sought to establish trust between management and unions. The USDOE's pledge to provide support to districts seeking to establish collaborative relationships served as a motivation for attendees. Despite the promised support for the initiative, some school districts such as the District of Columbia and New York City that had planned to attend were reported absent due to disagreements over teacher evaluation and layoff policies.

Teachers' unions agree that teacher evaluations are about improving the quality of teaching, not just rating teachers. After the Chicago Teachers' Union 2015 strike, for example, an unusual point of collaboration was the establishment of a joint committee with Chicago Public Schools to develop its teacher evaluation.

Positive Outcomes

Collaboration is a key ingredient to producing positive outcomes and has not disappointed in the area of teacher quality. Worth noting have been increased outcomes in student achievement, student graduation rates, and stakeholder collaboration. As a result, in school districts where collaboration between unions and management is the norm, there has been a decrease in the number of teacher terminations, something the unions laud and celebrate.

Let's look at Toledo, for instance, where the performance of students on standardized tests rose slightly as a result of the collaboration between the school district and the teachers' union on teacher quality (Eberts, 2007; Malin, 2014). Toledo ranked highest on the state-performance indices for grades three to six and boasted the highest graduation rate in the state as of 2013. Some researchers attributed Toledo's success to its use of peer review in place of traditional methods of evaluating teacher performance for more than three decades. In this particular jurisdiction, the collaboration on teacher evaluation reduced the number of terminations due to ineffectiveness. Under PAR, for example, first-year teachers and ineffective veteran teachers receive intensive support and evaluation through the collaboration between school administrators and consulting teachers. Referral for termination is a last resort in the PAR programs around the country.

Merit Pay

Merit pay and value-added measures of student achievement are generally not regarded as fair instruments to evaluate teachers because of the subjectivity of the instruments, at least from the point of view of teachers' unions and some researchers. They consider Cost of Living Adjustments (COLA) as fair mechanisms for compensating all educators. It was no wonder that anger over merit pay triggered the February 2019 Denver teachers' union strike. The same merit pay issues are enshrined in the IMPACT evaluation systems in the District of Columbia Public Schools and have led to an outcry from the union since the inception of the system (District of Columbia Public Schools, n.d.).

Some researchers expended a substantial amount of effort around collaboration on teacher quality as unions evolved from the industrial model of teacher unionism to a more solutions-oriented model that favored education reform. Union parent organizations, the AFT and the NEA, both support the collaborative model. In 1997, NEA president Bob Chase urged affiliates to embrace what he termed the *new unionism* in a remarkable shift from traditional bread-and-butter-focused unionism. Both parent organizations saw collaboration on teacher quality in particular as a way to move in the same direction, putting the education of kids front and center and creating the right learning environments for them.

Although the AFT and the NEA have traditionally not favored standardized testing as a measure of teacher effectiveness, the president of the AFT was instrumental in the development of the labor-management collaboration in Baltimore, Maryland; Pittsburgh, Pennsylvania; and New Haven, Connecticut. Each district reached a contract agreement, experimenting with new systems of teacher evaluation and pay based on measures of testing.

In examining the outcomes produced by labor-union collaboration, it is clear that there is no uniformity in implementation of collaborative partnerships. Notably, merit pay and value-added measures of student achievement (which are used to show what effects individual teachers have on student learning in a particular year) were used to evaluate teachers in some school districts such as Hillsborough, Florida; New Haven, Connecticut; and Winston-Salem/Forsyth, North Carolina. Other districts such as the ABC Unified School District (ABCUSD), California, and school districts in Douglas County, Colorado; Montgomery County, Maryland; Plattsburgh, New York; and St. Francis, Minnesota used peer evaluations instead of student test scores.

Being recognized as a successful and achieved teacher is tied in with the accountability measures that are in place to establish that determination. That accountability thus requires some type of mechanism using supervisors or peers to measure success. The U.S. Department of Education's RTTT deemed teacher evaluation a necessary reform initiative to improve teaching and learning, and that is why it saw collaboration between school districts and unions as an absolute necessity. Even though collective bargaining clauses in some districts did not require union involvement in the development of teacher evaluations, RTTT required that evaluation systems be "designed and developed with teacher and principal involvement" (Sims, 2015, p. 637). Teachers' unions agree that teacher evaluations are about improving the quality of teaching, not just rating teachers. This has led hardline leaders who have traditionally opposed teacher-evaluation reform to soften their positions.

Although the Chicago Teachers' Union (CTU) made news with an effective strike action in recent years, its collaboration with the Chicago Public Schools (CPS) to establish a joint committee to develop the evaluation system was a laudable effort within the education-reform community. Data obtained from teachers and school administrators between 2012 and 2014 revealed that in the first year of implementation, teachers were generally positive about the accuracy of the process and of the ratings that they received. It is not known at this moment how much the joint initiative has improved, but it was generally a step in the right direction to involve teachers in the decision-making process on their evaluations.

Jurisdictions that have adopted joint responsibility between school districts and unions on teacher evaluations have witnessed major successes in both teacher quality and their relationships with union members. Equal representation between school districts and their unions on evaluation teams has garnered trust over time, although in some jurisdictions there are discrepancies in the composition of teams. While some districts have been intentional in including principals on their teams because of the unique leadership role they play in a school, others believe that including principals could potentially increase adversarial relationships with the union, especially on decisions regarding the termination of a teacher's employment.

Fear Among Rank and File

Unions care about protections for their members and continue to advocate for due process rights and fair wages. These are some of the issues that have typically been the source of contentious relationships between them and management. Pivoting to a model where collaboration is the norm poses anxiety among rank and file as they deem that relationship to be too cozy and one that could result in an erosion of their bread-and-butter protections. Across the board, a collaborative teacher evaluation system such as PAR guarantees those protections even though the protections do not shield marginal teachers from termination. The termination of ineffective teachers makes a good case for opponents of teachers' unions who have traditionally accused the latter of protecting incompetent teachers and prioritizing their needs over the educational needs of their students. For these critics, shaming and demonizing unions over low student achievement rather than collaborating might result in a sense of urgency for their members to do better. Unfortunately, those antagonistic relationships instead erode the mutual trust that ought to exist between teachers and the public at large.

Effective Partnerships

Among the districts that have developed effective partnerships, six have been highlighted for adopting effective collaboration and joint responsibility regarding teacher evaluation and support. ABCUSD in California is known to have championed a peer-assistance mentoring, support, and evaluation program known as Peer Assistance Support System (PASS). In Hillsborough County, Florida Public Schools, even though a lack of funding thwarted earlier discussions in the 1990s, the district came together with the union to establish an extensive range of mentoring, PAR, and training opportunities for teachers and principals. These collaborative efforts of the district were rewarded by a multimillion dollar Intensive Partnership grant from the Bill and Melinda Gates Foundation to improve effective teaching. Norfolk School District, Virginia; Plattsburgh City Public School District, New York; St. Francis Independent School District, Minnesota; and Toledo City School District in Ohio established similar systems that set up joint responsibility between the union and the school district. The collaboration in Norfolk was very unique and stood out because Virginia is a right-to-work (RTW) state, which, like others, is not union-friendly. St. Francis involved three entities:

the union, the management, and the school board. The Student Improvement Performance Program (SIPP) in St. Francis included a peer-review component, a new teacher-induction program, and mentoring.

Montgomery County Public Schools (MCPS) in Maryland has developed an approach to collaboration that is considered one of the models in the country that is worth emulating. Their partnership epitomizes a reliable and effective labor-management collaboration on teacher evaluation that has been rare to come by both at the dawn of the century and contemporarily. PAR was instituted in 2000 and led to improved relations between the teachers' union and the school system based on mutual trust (Sullivan, 2012). This was the culmination of three decades of collaboration between the school district and the Montgomery County Education Association (MCEA) over teacher evaluations. Like most success stories of collaboration, the Montgomery County collaboration emanated from historical adversarial relationships similar to those in New York's Plattsburgh City Public School District in 1975.

During the 1970s and 1980s, MCEA used the industrial unions' approach to secure gains for teachers, notably through an eight-day strike. "The association, which had been a docile and largely irrelevant body before the 1960s, had become radicalized and developed into a forceful advocate for teacher needs and concerns" (Sullivan, 2012, p. 146). As the union developed in strength, it soon realized that it had a vision far beyond that of a trade union protecting its members. "The vision of teachers and administrators working as professional colleagues engaged in the task of improving education in the public schools remained alive in the minds of some teachers" (p. 146).

Consequently, the union sought to join the Teacher Union Reform Network (TURN), which had a goal of transforming teachers' unions into agents of reform. That mindset developed into panels and committees co-chaired by MCPS and MCEA that met for two years to create PAR. The fact that under the program, teachers and administrators were recognized as equal partners in assessing teacher effectiveness was a major milestone in labor-management relations. The partnership allowed for joint training between principals and consulting teachers to prepare them to conduct evaluations.

The Pittsburgh Public School (PPS) District story, where the partnership with the Pittsburgh Federation of Teachers (PFT) evolved into the establishment of a strong bond between two members of the leadership team, was even more compelling. Encouraged by the outcomes of their prior collaboration on professional development, the district's Chief Academic Officer convinced her counterpart within the union not to retire so they could revamp the teacher evaluation system.

The recognition that there would be a greater buy-in with the involvement of teachers in the process was a welcome move in the history of labor-management relations. The involvement of all upper-level administrators from the central office, the union, school administrators, and classroom teachers was a divergence from the common practice of top-down imposition by district leadership and led to greater trust, especially within union rank and file.

The ground-breaking collaboration between PPS and PFT inspired 28 schools to volunteer to pilot the program that became known as the *Research-Based Inclusion System of Evaluation* (RISE) upon final adoption (Hamill, 2011). The Pittsburgh partnership was significant evidence of the value of collaboration, especially when practitioners believe that their voices are heard and can influence district policy. Furthermore, those informal relationships of trust where a superintendent publicly declares that *"I don't go many days without talking to John (union president)"* (Hamill, 2011, p. 34) is a testament to the value of working together on an issue as sensitive to teachers as evaluation.

Taking joint responsibility for teacher quality is hailed not only by beneficiaries but also by education activists. AFT president Randi Weingarten argues that what matters in education is not so much about how the schools are managed but how much teachers are supported and provided a seat at the table to voice their opinions on education policy. She strongly advocated for PAR when it was introduced. Similarly, Adam Urbanski, the co-founder of TURN, continues to advocate for the recognition of accomplished teachers to support struggling teachers to help them achieve quality in the profession. As a practical matter, there is no better support than teachers learning from their peers. The social compact that colleagues establish over time working together creates a level of comfort that is not available with top-down support.

In terms of support, sharing a common vision and having joint responsibility on teacher evaluation benefit both novice and veteran teachers over time. In districts where collaboration on teacher evaluation is the norm, there is a decline in the number of terminations resulting from ineffectiveness because teachers deemed ineffective receive ongoing support. Under PAR, for example, first-year teachers and ineffective veteran teachers receive intensive support and evaluation through the collaboration between school administrators and consulting teachers. Referral for termination is a last resort in the PAR programs highlighted.

In Toledo, performance on standardized tests rose slightly as a result of the collaboration between the school district and the teachers' union on teacher quality. Toledo ranked highest on state performance indices for grades 3 to 6 and boasted the highest graduation rate in the state as of 2013. The positive results of the PAR program in Toledo encouraged other school districts in the state to adopt it.

Similarly, both teachers and management saw the effectiveness of the Montgomery County Peer Review program in establishing an equal partnership in the development and implementation of an evaluation system as a positive step toward improving not only teacher quality but also student learning.

The details provided in describing the Montgomery County program by researchers make a compelling case in favor of collaborative partnerships between school districts and teachers' unions due to the positive outcomes. In establishing the collaborative partnership, Montgomery County Public Schools teachers had a vision that was far beyond that of a trade union protecting its members from compensation and benefits issues. Sims (2015) posited that "the vision of teachers and administrators working as professional colleagues engaged in the task of improving education in the public schools remained alive in the minds of some teachers" (p. 146).

That the evaluation system was based on core principles including but not limited to a commitment to student learning, knowledge of subject matter, effective management of student learning, and efficient monitoring of student progress was a sign that the collaboration already anticipated outcomes that surpassed benefits to union members. The continuous support that both novice and veteran teachers received benefitted teacher satisfaction and retention.

Increases in student achievement also provided Toledo City School District and the Toledo Federation of Teachers a reason to celebrate their collaborative partnership. In the eyes of the union, it was more pertinent to defend the academic standards that it participated in developing than to protect its members. Per Malin (2014), "under peer review, the union is transformed from a protector of the irremediably incompetent to a defender of the professional standards that it participated in creating and administering" (p. 532). Furthermore, as with other peer-review systems around the country, the attrition rate for poor performers was higher than under traditional evaluation systems.

Indications are that the collaboration between school districts and teachers' unions on teacher quality ushered in a culture where teacher effectiveness and student performance became non-negotiables to the extent that nine states included student performance as a criterion for tenure and 20 included teacher ineffectiveness as grounds for dismissal. Some collaborations resulted in a restricted teacher labor market based on a credentialed pool of teachers who had gone through a standard license process. Having a full pool of credentialed, as opposed to noncredentialed, teachers had the potential for producing positive outcomes for student learning.

However, right-to-work laws dampened the momentum garnered by successes in collaborative partnerships to ensure better teacher quality. In states with right-to-work laws, there is a ban on collective bargaining, and any form of collaboration between unions and employers on conditions of employment is not guaranteed. In states such as California and Michigan, locals resisted the idea of collaborative partnerships; in Wisconsin and Idaho, legislative changes altered the dynamics and created more adversarial relationships with unions. Perhaps with intentional collaboration and trust-building between management and labor, the 2019 Los Angeles strike could have been averted.

In addition to Michigan and Wisconsin, Florida also prohibited bargaining on teacher evaluations. Wisconsin, in particular, drew national attention after Governor Scott Walker introduced legislation in 2011 that limited collective bargaining for most public employees to wages. Even though unions and their supporters staged a protest inside and outside the state capitol, the legislature still succeeded in passing the legislation, arguing that it was a money-saving measure.

Failed DC Experiment

In the District of Columbia Public Schools, the lack of teacher input in the development of the teacher evaluation system and the punitive effects of the evaluation system have resulted in ongoing low teacher morale and a lack of buy-in. While it is easy to put the blame solely on the pioneer schools' chancellor who developed the system without teacher or union input, the ultimate blame lies with the city's leadership and congress. Chancellor Rhee, in developing the IMPACT evaluation system, acted in compliance with a 1996 act of Congress that restricted teacher evaluations from collective bargaining. However, seeking the positive contributions of teachers and their union similar to those in other jurisdictions could have averted some of the initial and ongoing backlash. There is ample research to support the line of reasoning that unilaterally developed and implemented or imposed teacher evaluation systems negatively impact teacher morale over time, as is the case in DC after over a decade of implementation.

Both teachers and administrators have either been forced out of the system due to ineffectiveness or have left on their own accord because of the pressure or perceived inequities in the system as a whole. The outcry around the lack of support has left the union no other choice than to find creative ways to support its members. Yet, regardless of the level of support, there are insurmountable obstacles to getting the level of support that sets teachers up for success. Independent studies conducted by the University of Virginia and Brown University have touted the effectiveness of the evaluation system in developing effective teachers and separating ineffective ones. The only outlier has been a study conducted by the American University School of Education that found racial and gender bias against women of color to be a major flaw of the system. Although there has been an outcry from both the union and its allies over the ineffectiveness of the system, the school district continues to maintain it, making occasional annual revisions, but still not producing super teachers or closing the prevalent student achievement gaps.

While the two chancellors who championed the IMPACT evaluation system, Michelle Rhee and Kaya Henderson, have largely been silent about the evaluation instrument they introduced, one of its architects, Jason Kamras, now superintendent of Richmond, Virginia Public Schools, currently believes that his thinking on teacher evaluation has evolved. Without publicly disavowing his role in the creation of the evaluation system, it is evident from Kamras's failure to introduce it in Richmond that he finds it to be ineffective. According to a May 2018 news article in the *Richmond Times Dispatch*, the Richmond Public Schools Superintendent showed no signs of bringing IMPACT to Richmond (Mattingly, 2018).

What the Research and Collective Bargaining Agreements Reveal

Researchers who favor the involvement of teachers' unions in crafting evaluation systems argue that districts stand to lose more when they unilaterally initiate and implement this type of policy. Unions that are not involved in reforming evaluation systems are likely to devote their resources to disrupting the reforms rather than supporting them. After analyzing collective bargaining rights and teacher evaluation reforms from four different states, it is clear that after evaluating their teachers, as much as 73% of administrators failed to make recommendations for improvement, and even among those who made such recommendations, only 45% were useful. AFT's 2008 resolution urging its affiliates to consider the collaborative system, PAR, offers more value to teacher quality than one-sided evaluations that tend to be retaliatory in some cases.

Collective Bargaining Agreements between DC Public Schools and the Washington Teachers' Union, spanning 1968 to 2016, reveal that both parties agreed to collaborate on teacher quality to a limited extent. From 1968 to 1994, the parties could collaborate on teacher evaluation, but in the 1998 to 2001 collective bargaining agreement, U.S. Congress limited the ability of the union to be involved in the establishment of teacher evaluations. According to Article XVII (A), "U.S. Congress legislation determined that teacher evaluation shall henceforth be the sole responsibility of the school district" (Collective Bargaining Agreement, 1998, p. 17). The legislation in D.C. Code § 1-617.18 specifically states that

> Notwithstanding any other provision of law, rule, or regulation, during fiscal year 2006 and each succeeding fiscal year, the evaluation process and instruments for evaluating District of Columbia Public Schools employees shall be a non-negotiable item for collective bargaining purposes. (p. 17)

The legislation notwithstanding, the union is allowed to consult with the superintendent/chancellor before the implementation of any evaluation instrument. One would think that the school district would tap into the consultation piece, as a sign of good faith, to afford the union and its members the opportunity to contribute ideas to help with their own development, but that is not the reality.

During a lunch chat at the Washington Teachers' Union's 2019 Shared Vision Conference on February 16, 2019, D.C. Chancellor Lewis Ferebee touted his collaboration with the teachers' union in Indianapolis (where he previously served) to develop the teacher-evaluation system and left the door open to the same level of collaboration with the teachers' union in the District of Columbia. However, he did not keep to that promise, although both parties agreed to create a taskforce that would review the evaluation tool and offer suggestions for improving it. Still, the chancellor failed to keep to the commitment, but rather engaged an outside entity to conduct a review of the evaluation tool. On October 16, 2016, he announced via a mass email to all DCPS teachers that he would be launching a comprehensive review of IMPACT with an immediate focus on teacher evaluation, but not on the evaluation of other school staff. While DCPS engaged teachers using a survey for feedback, the Washington Teachers' Union, voicing its concern for teaching quality, continued to lobby a coalition of lawmakers to introduce legislation that would enable it to be able to negotiate the evaluation system for its members.

Despite the limitations on teacher evaluation, in past and current CBAs, both parties in the District of Columbia expressed the desire to collaborate on professional development. Both the school district and the teachers' union agreed in their collective bargaining agreements to a shared vision and philosophy on professional development. Article 2.3.1 of the 2016-2019 contract stipulates that

> The school district and the teachers' union agree that quality professional development for teachers is essential to promoting and sustaining high-quality teaching and learning in the classroom. The teachers' union is successfully collaborating and partnering with the school district to provide innovative and rigorous professional development for all bargaining unit teachers to promote student achievement. (Collective Bargaining Agreement, 2016, p. 14)

They also agreed to collaborate on the instructional coach model.

Teachers in the nation's capital generally agree that they are involved in several areas of teacher quality either through district-offered professional development or through direct collaboration with colleagues and school administrators. While some members of the teachers' union have referenced direct support from their administrators for various action research initiatives or the new teacher induction program, these are far from being systemwide.

As General Vice President (GVP) of the union prior to April 2021, the former president, Jacqueline Pogue Lyons, identified professional development as one of the areas in which the union and school district's collaboration was effective. In her dual role as GVP and professional development coordinator, she credited school administrators who were very accommodating in allowing the union to use their buildings to host professional development sessions for its members. Some school administrators who found value in the professional development opportunities offered by the union encouraged their teachers, especially those identified as developing under the teacher-evaluation system, to take advantage of such opportunities. It is well known within union ranks that when it comes to collaboration on teacher quality, different school administrators respond differently, prioritizing their individual schools' needs to contravening directives that might have been issued by their superiors. These tend to be the administrators who consider the union as a partner rather than feed into the adversarial narrative that is characteristic of some union-management relationships. For these school leaders, collaborating with the teachers' union on career advancement and leadership pipelines for teachers who stayed in the classroom would result in better educators and better outcomes for students at large.

For many years, teachers' unions have taken the lead in developing effective teachers through different initiatives and constantly seeking collaboration with districts. These initiatives have ranged from professional development opportunities to resource sharing and developing curricula. Developing effective teachers requires a collaborative approach that cannot simply be limited to districts and their unions, but also meaningful partnerships with university teacher preparation programs and other professional organizations. Students stand to benefit the most when they are taught by the most qualified and effective teachers who receive continuous support at all levels, whether that is through increased professional development offerings, professional development funds, negotiated time to seek out-of-district opportunities, or union and management putting aside their differences to do what is best for children.

Further Reading

Adnot, M., Dee, T., Katz, V., & Wyckoff, J. "Teacher Turnover, Teacher Quality, and Student Achievement in DCPS." National Bureau of Economic Research, March 1, 2017.

American Federation of Teachers. (n.d.). *AFT Teach.* https://www.aft.org/education/aft-teach

American Federation of Teachers. (n.d.). *Share My Lesson.* Retrieved June 3, 2025, from https://sharemylesson.com/

Anrig, G. (2014). Cultivating collaboration: The science behind thriving labor-management relationships. *American Educator, 37*(4), 4–13.

Bangs, J., & MacBeath, J. (2012). Collective leadership: the role of teacher unions in encouraging teachers to take the lead in their own learning and in teacher policy. *Professional Development in Education, 38*(2), 331–343. doi:10.1080/19415257.2012.65

Bleiberg, J., Brunner, E., Harbatkin, E., Karft, M.A., & Springer, M.G. (2021). *The effect of teacher evaluation on achievement and attainment: Evidence from statewide reforms.* Annenberg Brown University.

Bruno, R. (2015). Teachers unions at a fork in the road: Strike for America: Chicago teachers against austerity and how to jump-start your union: Lessons from the Chicago teachers. *New Labor Forum (Sage Publications Inc.), 24*(1), 116–119. https://doi.org/10.1177/1095796014560757

Campbell, C.M., Parker, C., Shand, R., Kelly-Massoud, A., Fashola, T., & Blanc, J. (2021). *Perspectives on DCPS IMPACT teacher evaluation system: Findings from teachers and school leaders.* American University School of Education.

Cavanagh, S. (2011). States urged to promote cooperation. *Education Week, 31*(12), S13–S14.

Collective Bargaining Agreement, Washington Teachers' Union-District of Columbia Public Schools, 1968–1969.

Collective Bargaining Agreement, Washington Teachers' Union-District of Columbia Public Schools, 1998–2001.

Collective Bargaining Agreement, Washington Teachers' Union-District of Columbia Public Schools, 2016–2019.

Coulson, A. J. (2010). The effects of teachers' unions on American education. *CATO Journal, 30*(1), 155–170.

Cowen, J. M., & Strunk, K. O. (2015). The impact of teachers' unions on educational outcomes: What we know and what we need to learn. *Economics of Education Review, 48*, 208–223.

Crabtree, P. (2016). Changing perspectives on teachers' unions. Retrieved from https://www.edweek.org/tm/articles/2016/04/01/changing-perspectives-on-teachers-unions.html?r=906222678#

Cunningham, P. (2014). An open letter to Randi Weingarten. *Education Week, 34*(11), 24–25.

District of Columbia Code § 1–617.18. Evaluation process for public school employees.

District of Columbia Public Schools. (n.d.). *IMPACT: The DCPS evaluation and feedback system for school-based personnel.* https://dcps.dc.gov/page/impact-dcps-evaluation-and-feedback-system-school-based-personnel

Downs, P. G. (2012). *The impact of school accountability laws on measures of trust between Indiana public school superintendents and teacher union leaders within the forum of mandatory discussion* (Ph.D.). Purdue University, United States: Indiana.

Durant, W. (1926). *The story of philosophy: The lives and opinions of the greater philosophers.* Simon and Schuster.

Eberts, R. W. (2007). Teachers unions and student performance: Help or hindrance? *Future of Children, 17*(1), 175–200.

Hamill, S. D. (2011). Pittsburgh's winning partnership. *American Educator, 35*(3), 28–34.

Honawar, V. (2007). Accords designed to turn around troubled schools. *Education Week, 26*(41), 1-15.

James, J. & Wyckoff, J. "Teacher Evaluation and Teacher Retention in DCPS." University of Virginia, January 2, 2019.

Lamagna, F. G. (2010). *Factors promoting and hindering collaboration in labor-management relations* (Ph.D.). Saybrook University, United States - California. Retrieved from https://search.proquest.com/dissertations/docview/761126867/abstract/E18D67A0F7F2403APQ/2

Lott, J., & Kenny, L. W. (2013). State teacher union strength and student achievement. *Economics of Education Review, 35*, 93–103. doi: 10.1016/j.econedurev.2013.03.006

Malin, M. H. (2014). Education reform and labor-management cooperation: What role for the law? *University of Toledo Law Review, 45*(3), 527–543.

Mattingly, J. (2018). *A 'culture of fear': How the teacher evaluation system Richmond's new superintendent created impacted D.C. schools (and why he won't bring it here).* Richmond: Time-Dispatch

Mirer, J. (2013). Right-to-work laws: History and fightback. *National Lawyers Guild Review, 70*(1), 30–40.

Paige, M. (2013). Applying the "paradox" theory: A law and policy analysis of collective bargaining rights and teacher evaluation reform from selected states. *Brigham Young University Education & Law Journal*, (1), 21–43.

Qazilbash, E. K. (2009, January 1). *Peer Assistance and Review: A cross-site study of labor-management collaboration required for program success.* ProQuest LLC. *relations.* Saybrook University, United States—California. Retrieved from https://search.proquest.com/dissertations/docview/

Rubinstein, S. A., McCarthy, J. E., & Center for American Progress. (2011). *Reforming public school systems through sustained union-management collaboration.* Center for American Progress.

Sawchuk, S. (2011b). New attitudes shaping labor-district relations. *Education Week, 31*(12), S2–S5.

Sawchuk, S., & Heitin, L. (2014). AFT, NEA agendas converge as external, internal pressures rise. *Education Week, 33*(37), 1–11.

ShareMyLesson. (n.d.). *ShareMyLesson.* Retrieved June 3, 2025, from https://sharemylesson.com/

Simon, M. (2012). A tale of two districts. *Educational Leadership, 70*(3), 58–63.

Sims, M. L. (2015). The business of teaching: Can a new contract change the culture? *Columbia Journal of Law & Social Problems, 48*(4), 605–652.

Spector, S. (2013). Cultivating labor management collaboration. *Leadership, 42*(5), 16–19.

Sporte, S. E., Jiang, J. Y., Luppescu, S., & Society for Research on Educational Effectiveness (SREE). (2014). *Teacher evaluation in practice: Understanding evaluator reliability and teacher engagement in Chicago Public Schools.* Society for Research on Educational Effectiveness.

Sullivan, T. D. (2009). *New unionism: The changing attitudes of union membership* (Ed.D.). University of Massachusetts Lowell, United States—Massachusetts. Retrieved from https://search.proquest.com/dissertations/docview/304917273/abstract/5A383302DC5240C9PQ/23

Sullivan, J. P. (2012). A collaborative effort: Peer review and the history of teacher evaluations in Montgomery County, Maryland. *Harvard Educational Review, 82*(1), 142–152.

Sustar, L. (2013). Teachers' unions at the crossroads: Can the assault on teachers be rebuffed? *New Labor Forum (Sage Publications Inc.), 22*(2), 60–68. doi:10.1177/10957960134832

Urbanski, A., Alves, T., & Bernstein, E. (2017). Give teachers a voice in education reform: Four principles for a more robust public education system. *Education Week 27*(13), 22–23.

Vachon, T. E., & Ma, J. (2015). Bargaining for success: Examining the relationship between teacher unions and student achievement. *Sociological Forum, 30*(2), 391–414. https://doi.org/10.1111/socf.12168

Weingarten, R. (2011). Voicing concerns, crafting solutions: Unions in the age of teacher bashing. *Education Review, 24*(1), 41–48.

CHAPTER 3

I Found My Voice

Coming together is the beginning. Keeping together is progress. Working together is success.

— Henry Ford

On a mild fall day, at Kaiser Permanente's Center for Total Health in the Capitol Hill neighborhood in the nation's capital, the bright rays of the morning sun filtered through the clear glass windows. At the sign-in desk of the facility, volunteers' faces beamed like the morning sun as local union leaders staggered in, eager to learn their new duties and responsibilities and engage with other union leaders at the annual Union Leadership Institute (ULI).

As volunteers helped members sign in and handed them their tote bags of swag, a pair of professionally dressed field representatives, coffee mugs in hand, welcomed them and ushered them to their seats. Among the newly elected school leaders, a shy-looking middle-aged African American woman keenly listened to speaker after speaker, until one topic hit close to home for her—her involvement in union activities at her school. She raised her hand, stoically took the microphone and calmly and passionately made her point, sobbing in between her testimony. "I found my voice," she said after recounting the story of how her school leader had attempted to silence and stymie her union activism after she called out injustices perpetuated toward students and staff at her school.

This is one out of thousands of stories recounted by teachers' union members across the country. Teachers fundamentally want to have a say in decision-making, and the fact that leadership at some campuses believes that top-down decision-making should be the norm is incomprehensible to those who genuinely care about the education of kids. The business of educating kids is not a one-person show; neither can a group of individuals pretend to know it all. Educating kids is a collective effort involving all stakeholders, teachers being the most important of them.

For its years in existence, the Washington Teachers' Union like other teachers' unions has stimulated "teacher voice" through various initiatives in which teachers take the lead, as well as through union-organized events such as the Union Leadership Institute, the Shared Vision Conference, monthly representative assembly meetings, participation on various committees, and testifying at different levels of government to influence policy. Additionally, teachers are regularly polled to seek their input on issues affecting them as union members. Teacher voice focuses on providing every teacher an opportunity to provide input into the choice of curriculum, the length of the school day, professional development, and teacher evaluation, among other issues.

In the past, depending on the jurisdiction, teachers and management have worked together on different initiatives, all with the goal of providing a quality education for students including the development of evaluation instruments. Empowered by their parent organizations, local unions and schools have collaborated on the budget process, for example. This level of collaboration is not the norm and is limited to a handful of districts. The superintendent of Jefferson County Public Schools, WV, and the union president collaborated on a budget process that involved all stakeholders reaching an agreement that cut 200 positions through attrition, instituted two furlough days, eliminated four professional development days, set a percent wage reduction for teachers, closed two schools, and imposed new transportation fees for parents.

Teacher voice is associated with decision-making and consultation at the local and district levels. Research respondents (school administrators and teachers) in a 2018 study acknowledged that teacher voice was indispensable to the decisions made at the school level. One school principal explained that she always invited the union building representative to look at what she was doing, shared with stakeholders, and provided feedback on what others might think once they introduced the program.

In her opinion, such an approach served the best interest of the school and reduced the number of grievances that teachers filed against her. Another principal argued that if the teachers were part of the decision-making process from the beginning to the middle and the end, including reflection and reevaluation, there would be more buy-in.

Conversely, some school leaders do the bare minimum to respect the collective bargaining agreement but make unilateral decisions because they believe by virtue of their training and roles as school leaders, it is their main responsibility to make decisions on what they believe is right for students. The principal of a prominent middle school in Washington, D.C. admitted that teacher voice was important in making decisions at her school, but when asked how union-management collaboration influenced policies at her school, she responded, "I read the contract; I don't want to violate the contract. I'm aware of the contract. Outside of that, I make decisions that I think are best for teachers and students within the building." This mindset is contrary to what meaningful collaboration is and deepens the suspicions that teachers, not only those who are part of a union, have for school leaders. Leaders with this mindset contribute to the constant calls from teachers' unions to create opportunities where teachers feel heard, play an active role in decision-making, and feel a sense of belonging in their respective educational communities. In an environment where everyone feels their voice matters, they are more likely to invest more time, leading to improved outcomes for their students. On the contrary, in work environments that are characterized by top-down leadership, low morale and low retention are commonplace and ultimately, students and families suffer the negative consequences when this occurs.

Embedded in the District of Columbia union's collective bargaining agreement are opportunities for teachers to collaborate with school leaders on the implementation of the agreement through local structures such as the School Chapter Advisory Committee, the Local School Advisory Team, the Personnel Committee, the Morning Block team, and the Student Behavior Management Committee. Where properly implemented, these Committees have been successful in shaping the decision-making culture in many buildings, but the climate in some buildings remains toxic and results in high teacher turnover. Collaboration, with opportunities for teachers to use their positive contributions to improve building culture without the fear of retaliation, could make a difference in what has traditionally been a culture of one-sided decision-making.

In one D.C. high school, the principal frequently invited her union building representative to review initiatives and share them with other members of the union for feedback. Such an approach, in her opinion, had the benefit of garnering buy-in and provided the teachers with the opportunity to take ownership both for the successes and failures of the initiatives. In the event where the outcome turned out to be unfavorable, both parties would have the chance to get back together to reevaluate and make amends. When parties genuinely engage in collaborative partnerships, there is no finger pointing when there are failures, and everyone returns to the table to either celebrate successes or to openly take ownership and make changes when things fail to go as intended.

There is ample evidence that there would be more buy-in when union members are involved in decision-making as demonstrated by participants that I interviewed for a 2018 study. A District of Columbia Public School administrator acknowledged not only that the union members at her school influenced decision-making at the local school level, but that they also were thought partners in strategizing on how to influence what happened at the district level that could benefit their local school community. In her words:

> Whenever I have a decision that I want to make about the school, I involve the members of the union, my School Chapter Advisory Committee (SCAC), and Local School Advisory Team (LSAT) to give input so that we could determine what's in the best interest of the school. Even though we know that principals usually have the final say in decision-making, I use a collaborative approach where we come together to decide what's in the best interest given the parameters that we may have at the district level. (Ngwa, 2018)

The Washington Teachers Union was involved in developing the selection criteria for the current school's chancellor. Even though the District did not respect the process with fidelity, the presence of four union members on the panel was a step in the right direction.

Effects of Janus v. AFSCME

The National Labor Relations Act (NLRA) of 1935 was enacted to protect the rights of employees and employers, encouraging both parties to collectively bargain, yet the latter has for decades put the former in a position where they have to continuously fight to make their voices heard in the workplace. Since the ruling on the *Janus v. American Federation of State, County, and Municipal Employees (AFSCME)* in June 2018, there have been renewed efforts by anti-union groups to undermine the rights afforded employees by the NLRA through their unions. In a five-to-four decision, the Supreme Court ruled in favor of Mark Janus, the plaintiff in the lawsuit, with conservative Justice Alito delivering the majority opinion of the Court. Prior to the ruling, Illinois law, like that of other jurisdictions in the country, compelled public employees to subsidize a union using what they called agency fees, even if they choose not to become members. The decision in the case was based on a violation of the free speech rights of union members, as they were compelled to make contributions that they did not consent to. The Court's decision that public sector unions could not charge fees to employees who declined to join unions meant that unions' revenues would substantially decrease, especially given that they would still be required to protect the rights of non-members under their respective collective bargaining agreements.

Before the ruling was delivered, national and local unions had been bracing for devastating effects, and so they prepared a path and strategy to handle the outcomes. According to the unions, five years after the decision, unions have seen a reversal of the intended outcomes, especially among teachers' unions around the country. In the immediate aftermath of the decision, CBS News published data depicting a sharp decline in the country's unionization rate by almost half between the 1980s and 2018, although there was also evidence that public employee unions were more resilient than those of the private sector. Public approval of labor unions has also witnessed a drastic surge since 2009 in spite of the Supreme Court's ruling. AFT membership for example grew by almost 100,000 members by July of 2024. Before the decision, membership was at 1.7 million, but through aggressive organizing efforts, the union was able to organize 185 new units in just two years between July 2022 and July 2024, increasing its membership numbers to slightly above 1.8 million.

The organizing efforts that led to strikes in unlikely states including West Virginia, Oklahoma, and Arizona were unprecedented and inconceivable. The uptick in teacher union strikes could be credited to the organizing efforts of teachers—not necessarily those with affiliations to a union—across the states, including in the most anti-union regions of the country, and became a galvanizing force for unions to support the efforts to make their voices heard. Teachers' unions used the decision in *Janus* as a rallying call for their members to reclaim their voices and rights. New teachers and former agency fee-paying members signed up for membership in record numbers because they understood what was at stake. Any organizer would tell you it takes seven attempts to convince a nonmember to join the union. The fact that they are joining on their own speaks for itself. No wonder, in the months following the *Janus* decision, teachers' unions saw an uptick in the number of new teachers signing up for membership at new teacher orientation ceremonies. This was the case at DC Public Schools New Educator Orientations (NEO), annual events co-sponsored by the school district and its union counterpart. From the 2018 event to date, a record number of new teachers have walked up to organizers, asking to sign up for membership. At the 2018 orientation alone, as I tracked the numbers as they came in, over 400 new educators signed up for union membership by the end of the event. In a strange show of solidarity, then-principal of Excel Academy and principal of the year, Tenia Pritchard, included in her remarks an encouragement to get new teachers to join their local union. The WTU recorded similar numbers during the August and September 2019 NEO and subsequent years. When asked why he joined the union, Tim Arrington, a third-grade special education teacher at Leckie Elementary School, stated the following as his reason: "A union empowers teachers and gives us a voice. Teaching is difficult work, and it's nice to know there's a support system." Jade

Dwelley, a social worker at Kramer middle school on her part stated that "it's good to have a large group of people who are supportive and to know that you have a sounding board, especially as a first-year social worker in a school. It's good to know that someone has my back."

Member Organizing Institute

For the WTU, it has not been business as usual post-*Janus*. The local reimagined itself in the face of adversity caused by the *Janus* decision. Prior to the *Janus* ruling, the revenue generated from agency fees accounted for a substantial portion of the budget. The time devoted to providing services to members, including pursuing grievances, administering dental and vison benefits, maintaining the sick leave and maternity and paternity banks, and working on other membership benefits, gave some members the impression that the union was a service provider. Yes, unions ensure that there is fairness and job protections for all, but in the wake of the threats posed by the Supreme Court ruling, it became increasingly clear that the union needed to return to the fundamentals of organized labor which is its power to effectively organize. One of the unique characteristics of the AFT is its conscious ability to provide grants to support its locals, and at this critical juncture when public employee unions faced the risk of diminishing power, it found the need to grow more organizers. The AFT made grants available to its locals through the Member Organizing Institute (MOI) to support its locals in their organizing efforts. In the spring of 2019, the WTU took advantage of the grant to hire part-time organizers from its membership to galvanize its organizing efforts.

The ten members who took advantage of the opportunity qualified through a rigorous selection process and training. This was the union's way of further empowering its members and giving them a voice and leadership roles. Members of the institute underwent coaching, role play, and supervised field work. From the spring through the summer, the member organizers were involved in a plethora of organizing efforts—knocking on doors after school and during their spring break, pursuing potential members at various schools to sign up for membership, turning up crowds for rallies, collecting petitions on behalf of the union, and even testifying before the city council on behalf of their union. By the time this cohort of organizers exhausted the term of their ten-week contract, some of them had distinguished themselves among rank and file. Maxine Elbert was featured on the front page of the *Washington Post* after a rally on school funding and went on to be appointed on the contract negotiating team with another member of the cohort; another was elected to serve on the executive board; and the others became more active than they previously were.

For the union leadership, the goal of the MOI was to prepare cohorts of activists to take the lead in key initiatives and to empower them to be change agents within the membership. In December 2019, a second cohort of eight organizers was recruited to play the same role as their predecessors had, while the latter served as mentors.

The organizing efforts of the local yielded a lot of fruits, with some within rank and file becoming more aware of how to leverage their voices and making an impact through various forms of activism including challenging and holding their current leadership more accountable.

Union Leadership Institute

With the new direction that the union was taking, every aspect of its initiatives needed transformation. When I was hired in July 2018 as Executive Director, one of my multiple responsibilities was the organization of the Union Leadership Institute (ULI) that typically took place in September and in January. Even though we changed the facilitation of the institute to include a mix of local union leaders from the schools and guest facilitators from the AFT and other partner organizations, a lot of the agenda maintained the status quo in terms of content. That content was centered to a greater extent on the service model of union operations—access to fringe benefits, the grievance process, compensation, etc. Upon reflection of my first year in the new role, I made the recommendation that the ULI be termed the Union Organizing Institute. Although the change of name did not go into effect, its content was different. The organizing department of AFT provided support in the organization of the fall 2019 ULI. Two organizers were assigned to partner with our field services specialists to provide organizing training to the local school union leaders on understanding power; organizing through leadership; building power and affinity through one-on-one conversations; and using lists, charts, and maps to conduct such conversations. In January 2020, I organized the second part of the ULI to focus on the same goals as the first one. The only addition this time around was that another element, Issues-Based Organizing, was added to the training agenda. The reviews from participants at both trainings were astounding and encouraging. When asked to share what motivated them to be part of the union, participants shared the following, among other reasons:

> *"I do this work because I believe change happens from the bottom up and not from the top."*
>
> *"My heart is with children. I've always advocated for children. I want to serve the people in my building who are serving the children."*
>
> *"We need a seat at the table."*
>
> *"I get extremely angry because I believe that we can do better."*
>
> *"I work too hard to be taken advantage of."*
>
> *"I'm here to fight for the rights of my students and teachers."*

It is worth mentioning here that prior to this training, I had recommended one of the field services specialists to attend a five-day *Essential Skills for Organizers—Part 1* program organized by the AFT at the Maritime Institute in Linthicum, Maryland. In January 2020, she returned for another five days for the second part of the same program.

The labor movement in general has survived over the decades due on the collective efforts of members using their voices in various ways to achieve results for themselves, whether that is through protests or strike actions. *Organized labor*, as the movement is generally referred to, involves groups of employees coming together as unions in different sectors to use their voices to make changes to their working conditions. In the case of teachers' unions, they find voices when they are able to advocate for themselves, their students, and their communities.

Empowering Others to Find Their Voice

In the heart of the upscale neighborhood of Georgetown that is home to Georgetown University is the prestigious Duke Ellington School of the Arts (DESA). The school has produced famous artists such as Dave Chappelle and Michaela Davis, among others. Although the school is considered part DC Public Schools (DCPS), the governance and employment structure are different from that of other schools within the district. As general background, according to a description of the school's governance, public and private partnerships have supported the school. From 2000, it evolved into what is known as the Duke Ellington School of the Arts Project (DESAP), which includes DCPS, the Ellington Fund, the Kennedy Center, and George Washington University. In 2020, two years after the *Janus* decision, the WTU did a preliminary analysis of the organizational structure at DESA and found that an estimated 75% of its operating budget was provided by DCPS while the remaining 25% came in through the Duke Ellington Fund. Management of the school is overseen by a board of directors, a structure that is not common in other DC public schools. This unique management structure of the school means that all its employees are likely not to be directly employed by DCPS whose employees legally fall under the WTU bargaining unit.

Because of this, WTU leadership believed it would in the best interest of all the teachers (musicians) at Duke Ellington to be organized under their bargaining unit, a process that appeared to be more complicated than it seemed, given the management structure, especially from a compensation standpoint. The first consideration was engaging the DC Council to pass legislation that would change the structure of the school, which would be the most direct pathway to organizing all the teachers. For WTU, it was a matter of fairness and equity, and engaging stakeholder groups including union and non-union members at the school, members of the board of directors, alumni, and union partners was critical in meeting these goals. Another option on the table was starting with the DC Public Employee Relations Board (PERB) and then moving it to the National Labor Relations Board, pitching it to these entities as a case of discrimination and seeking to protect and uphold the rights of the affected teachers to organize. The key evidence to be presented would be the discrepancy in the pay structure. Despite all the strategizing and brainstorming with allies and legal experts, and as well intended as it sounded, the initiative did not go anywhere.

In the same situation as DESA teachers were teachers in the district's public charter schools. Even though the latter receive public funding from the DC government, they are held to different accountability standards, and their teachers have limited job protections due to the lack of collective bargaining. Charter school teachers are at-will employees and can be terminated without cause. Current DC legislation allows for charter schools to receive the same percentage of salary increases that union members of the WTU bargaining unit receive when they ratify a new contract. However, there is no requirement or guarantee that the money would be used toward teacher salaries at the charter schools. Similarly, unlike in unionized schools, charter school teachers and staff are not guaranteed a say in decision-making, unlike in DCPS schools where some mandatory structures for stakeholder engagement exist. The WTU thus found itself to be well-positioned to take on elevating the voices of teachers in the charter school system by bringing them under their bargaining unit. The initial thoughts were centered around the formation of a coalition with other public sector employee unions such as the Service Employees International Union (SEIU), and the American Federation of State, County and Municipal Employees (AFSCME) to lobby the DC Council to extend the same rights that they possessed to public charter school employees. Just like the DESA situation, this would have involved passing legislation, submitting an organizing plan to the AFT, or engaging the NLRB. The AFT has however maintained its aggressive efforts to unionize charter schools in the nation's capital. Previous attempts at Paul Charter School in 2017 failed, while a successful vote by teachers at Cézar Chávez Public Charter School ended up not giving the voice that teachers deserved as the campus closed its doors. Although the charter operator attributed the closure to declining enrollment, the theory among teachers and the union movement was that it was a retaliatory move to avoid giving teachers a say in decision-making and holding the leadership accountable. One would have thought that wanting to plant the seeds of a union at the campus was aligned with the social justice values held by the person for which the school was named.

There was however a glimmer of hope when the AFT successfully helped to organize Mundo Verde Bilingual Public Charter School, making it the first charter school in the city with a teachers' union. The rising costs of healthcare and notably a request from the school's administration for staff to contribute more toward their healthcare served as rallying forces which led them to request more input into decision-making at the school. A ratified union contract guaranteed the teachers not only the right to have a voice in decision-making but also salary raises through a negotiated process. Just like the case of Cézar Chávez, a second newly opened campus, Calle Ocho, successfully joined the union but, not long after that, management closed it down. That closure was blamed on the COVID-19 pandemic.

As the pandemic ravaged the nation, and as teachers and other school staff struggled to seek health protections before returning to school buildings through their unions, teachers in charter schools were left without a voice. While members of the WTU actively negotiated a health and safety memorandum with DCPS for a safe return to in-person learning, schools without a union were left with no voice. It is no doubt that there was greater energy and motivation for more charter schools to want to form a union post-pandemic. The AFT now boasts of more than 1,200 teachers and staff at more than 16 charter schools having organized with them since the start of the 2022–23 school year. Among these were DC International School (DCI) and Capital City Charter School, the latter voting in May 2024 to join a union under their bargaining agent, District of Columbia Alliance of Charter Teachers and Staff, DC ACTs, which is an affiliate of AFT just like the WTU.

In recent years, other community groups have joined the fight for empowering teachers to have more voice at the workplace, which stretches beyond working conditions. Among these groups is EmpowerEd. Although not a teachers' union, the founder of this advocacy group left the local DC Public School as a union-building representative to start this advocacy group. The group has benefitted from the support of former Montgomery County Teachers' Association president Mark Simon, former DC Board of Education (DCBOE) president Ruth Wattenberg, and former ward 8 DCBOE member Markus Batchelor. When one of DCPS's local schools, Dunbar HS, was involved in a grading scandal in 2018, Scott Goldstein, EmpowerEd's executive director, partnered with the WTU to give voice to the teachers who were witch-hunted in the scandal. His teacher voice summit is gradually gaining ground among both traditional and charter school teachers. Scott's presence is felt at stakeholder meetings. Public testimony at the DC Council of the DCSBOE is relentless, and Scott encourages and empowers educators from both the charter and traditional public schools to take an active role in elevating their voices in the policy sphere.

Through survey instruments, he is able to capture the perceptions of teachers/educators on wellbeing and retention issues and then uses the results to advocate on their behalf. Like organized labor organizations, his organization believes that greater teacher voice and wellness will lead to a higher retention rate in the city's K–12 schools. Whether that voice is in the way educators are evaluated, compensated, or supported in other aspects of their job performance, the issues are the same issues that the teachers' union cares about. As well-intended as the organization's initiatives are, some union leaders believe the organization's work conflicts with the organizing work of the legal bargaining agent of the public schools' teachers in the city. However, the organization is registered as a nonprofit and does not collect dues from teachers but rather benefits from donations and other privileges afforded to similar organizations.

The push for teacher voice has not come without controversy, although such controversy has perhaps not been verbalized or made public. Union affiliates like their parent organizations rely on member dues to effectively render services to their members. Because of the financial responsibilities that the affiliates owe to the parent organization through monthly per capita dues, the WTU, at least internally, had argued that they should be at the forefront of charter school organizing. When the AFT stepped in to help Mundo Verde organize as a means of giving them a voice in decision-making at the workplace, the WTU believed it should rightfully represent the school as the bargaining agent by virtue of its geographic location. Whether that line of thinking ever made its way to AFT leadership remains a matter of conjecture. It is not known how much energy or resources the current WTU leadership invests in charter school organizing, but the fact that it stands in solidarity with the schools that recently unionized is a sign of unity. "I'm thrilled that these charter school educators will be getting a seat at the table to have an avenue to access the respect, rights, and resources that they need for themselves and their students," (American Federation of Teachers, 2024) Jacqueline Pogue Lyons, former WTU president is quoted to have expressed after the unionization victories at DCI and Capital City Charter School.

No matter what it takes for any individual educator or group of educators to have a voice in school governance, the choice of curriculum, or the respect that they need to perform their job duties, the ultimate beneficiaries are the students. There is a correlation between teachers' participation in decision-making and high retention rates as studies have found. What remains a problem is that there is no organic involvement of teachers in decision-making. When school leaders do not feel the need to elevate teacher voice as part of the school culture, but rather do so because they are compelled to by the provisions of the collective bargaining agreement, the resultant effect is a breakdown in trust and low morale. The stories of unionization efforts to give teachers a seat at the table are very compelling and exciting to hear, but what remains to be seen is the good faith involved in taking teachers' viewpoints into consideration when making instructional and organizational decisions at the school level. Every member of an organized labor group agrees that their union plays a critical role in elevating their voices as we notice with the organizing efforts of teachers' unions. The ability of organized labor to sit across the table to bargain on behalf of its members is very empowering. Without this, decision-making is top-down, fairness is a myth, and the workplace is a toxic environment where retaliation for standing up for what is right is commonplace. The role of teachers' unions in seeking long-lasting partnerships and coalitions to create a platform where their members feel seen and heard cannot be overemphasized.

Further Reading

American Federation of Teachers. (2024). *Second D.C. public charter school in a week votes to unionize with DC ACTS.* https://www.aft.org/press-release/second-dc-public-charter-school-week-votes-unionize-dc-acts

Anrig, G. (2014). Cultivating collaboration: The science behind thriving labor-management relationships. *American Educator, 37*(4), 4–13.

Collective Bargaining Agreement, Washington Teachers' Union-District of Columbia Public School District (1998–2001).

Collective Bargaining Agreement, Washington Teachers' Union-District of Columbia Public Schools, 2016–2019.

Collins, Sam P.K.(2023): "Matching Teachers' Funds Raises Questions of Public Charter School Unions." *Washington Informer.*

Howell, C.D. & Schmitzer, C. (2022). Online and the picket line: West Virginia teachers' use of an online community to organize. *Critical Education, 13*(2), 59–76.

Irvanova, Irina (2019): "Union membership in the U.S. hit record low in 2018." *CBS News.*

Janus v. American Federation of State, County, and Municipal Employees, Council 31, 138 S. Ct. 2448 (2018).

Maton, R. (2022). "We're ready to fight": The story of a protest movement. *Critical Education, 13*(4), 42–49. https://newlaborforum.cuny.edu/2020/10/03/the-red-for-ed-movement-two-years-in/

Ngwa, T.C. (2018) *Fostering organizational change through a solutions-driven culture of collaboration. A case study of a teachers' union in the mid-Atlantic region.* ProQuest LLC.

Sawchuk, S. (2013). District-union partnership. *Education Week, 32*(20), S16–S18.

Stark, L.W., Dyke, E. & Maton, R. (2022). Afterword: Reflections on contemporary educator movements. *Critical Education, 13*(4), 50–57.

Tarlau, R. (2023). Networked movements and bureaucratic unions: The structure of the 2018 #RedForEd teachers' strikes. *ILR Review, 76*(5), 833–863.

Ukhun, Kelley (2024): "Capital City Public Charter School in D.C. Votes for a Voice on the Job." AFT Press Release – www.aft.org

Urbanski, A., Alves, T., & Bernstein, E. (2017). Give teachers a voice in education reform: Four principles for a more robust public education system. *Education Week 27*(13), 22–23.

U.S. Congress. (1935). National Labor Relations Act, 29 U.S.C. §§ 151-169.

Weingarten, R. (2011). Voicing concerns, crafting solutions: Unions in the age of teacher bashing. *Education Review, 24*(1), 41–48.

CHAPTER 4

We Can Do Better

I can do things you cannot; you can do things I cannot; together we can do great things.

— Mother Teresa

The business of improving students' social, emotional, and academic outcomes cannot and should not be the sole responsibility of teachers and education leaders. The saying that "it takes a village to raise a child" should apply to education the same way it applies to our respective local communities. Despite continuous calls for collaboration among stakeholders, some school districts continue to resist meaningful collaboration, but in other districts, individual schools and their unions have worked together to turn around failing schools. If General Motors and the United Auto Workers could put their historical differences aside in order to jointly build a plant in Tennessee in the 1980s, why can school districts and their union partners not do the same? Numerous research studies have demonstrated that when it comes to student outcomes, more gains would be made with the participation of both labor and management than with only top-down management mandates. In fact, Cunningham (2014) made the case that:

> Reasonable people on all sides of the education debate understand that, even if we don't always agree on the path forward, we mostly want the same thing: more young people with the education they need, more schools and teachers with the resources and respect they need and deserve, and greater public confidence in education. When we reach that end zone, we can all dance together. (p. 3)

In the history of education reform, the 2002 No Child Left Behind (NCLB) legislation and the 2009 Race to the Top (RTTT) initiative made student achievement the cornerstone of what schools and school districts were to achieve. The threat of closing failing schools under NCLB forced both labor and management to engage in meaningful partnerships with the goal of reaching adequate yearly progress (AYP). The quest for more funding under RTTT incentivized districts and states to engage in meaningful reform to increase student achievement. It was not uncommon to hear education commentators state that "if there is something good coming out of NCLB, it is more union-management collaboration on student achievement" (Honowar, 2017). Empirical evidence obtained from Indiana Public School Districts supported the opinions of these commentators. In a quantitative study involving 50 schools' superintendents in Indiana, the author used a survey instrument to determine how the stress of punitive consequences impacted the relationship between the superintendents and teachers. One of the survey questions specifically asked for the superintendents' opinions of perceived change in cooperation in their relationships with their teachers' unions. The researchers determined in their findings that there was collaboration to improve student outcomes, especially in failing schools, thanks to accountability laws mandated by NCLB.

In an *Education Week* article, Honawar (2007) identified accords that sought to turn around failing schools under NCLB, noting the unusual collaboration between the teachers' union and Annapolis High School in Maryland in the commentary. Under the terms of the agreement, the teachers' union and the district committed to working together to raise student achievement, tying bonuses to the anticipated achievement, and the teachers in return committed to working at the school for at least three additional years. With the frequent teacher turnover in schools around the country, there couldn't have been a better point of agreement than one that guaranteed teacher retention.

Similar partnership agreements were reached in Cleveland to raise the test scores of third graders within three years. In the Miami Dade area, the two stakeholders worked on school improvement plans for the 39 lowest-performing schools (Honawar, 2007). In Chicago, the collaboration known as the "Fresh Start Program" was enacted in 2005 to help revamp eight schools that NCLB identified as failing (Honawar, 2007). The role played by Chicago teachers in decision-making helped to change the mindsets within the union rank and file and resulted in four of the schools being removed from the probation list. National legislation on education reform has had its flaws and has failed to achieve its intended goals, leading critics to question whether legislation is warranted to improve student outcomes. Yet, in the examples cited above, the silver lining has been the unprecedented and welcome collaboration between teachers' unions and districts to attempt solutions to raising student achievement. Legislation notwithstanding, unions have always sought collaboration with stakeholders to help resolve the nation's k–12 education problems.

Inspired by the different pieces of legislation on education, the USDOE under the Obama Administration more than ever saw itself highlighting greater collaboration geared at improving student achievement. The Department also organized conferences aimed at building relationships of trust between management and unions with the goal that such trust would lead to better student outcomes. At such conferences, teams made up of superintendents, school boards, and unions found themselves in the same room working toward the same goals and backed not only by the USDOE but also by private foundations that generally were not union allies.

In a mixed study conducted by Rubinstein and McCarthy in 2016, the researchers offered strong evidence that both institutional partnerships and school-level collaboration led to significant gains in student performance. Using data from surveys, interviews, and student performance from a sample of 27 schools in the ABC Unified School District (ABCUSD), the authors found that schools with stronger partnerships scored significantly higher on the California standardized achievement test. The researchers intimated that despite the high poverty levels of the schools sampled, the students produced high results, which they attributed to collaborative partnerships.

These findings stood in stark contradiction to those of scholars who suggested that the presence of unions was an obstacle to student achievement. Previous findings, contradictory to those from ABCUSD, came from Lott and Kenny in 2013, who used a quantitative study of 721 school districts in 42 states to examine the impact of contributions made by state teachers' unions on student test scores. The researchers performed an analysis of financial data from this sample to conclude that unions were stronger in states with high union dues and spending. Consequently, the unions in these states negotiated contracts that provided protections for inept teachers. These contracts, they argued, negatively impacted student achievement in math and reading. However, the researchers did not provide any findings to support the assumption that labor-management collaboration negatively impacted student achievement; neither did they cite any existing literature to corroborate this school of thought.

Even though Cowen and Strunk (2015) suggested in their findings that stronger collective bargaining agreements (CBA) and unions resulted in lower student achievement and lower graduation rates, they also found that students in unionized school districts performed better than their peers in non-unionized school districts. The mixed findings made it difficult to corroborate the findings of Lott and Kenny on student achievement. Earlier, in 2012, Bangs and MacBeath made the case for the benefits of ongoing accords between management and unions concerning student achievement despite a history of conflict between the two. The authors went further to contend that countries such as Finland, with the highest student performance, also had strong teachers' unions whose members were treated as partners with management to achieve better student outcomes.

Even though the findings of a single case study on labor-management relations in 2010 by Lamagna that sought to explore the factors promoting and hindering collaboration characterized those relations as evolving, the strongest conclusion supporting collaboration concerned student achievement. Half the labor participants and one-third of management participants agreed that focusing on students would increase collaboration between the two entities. In the participants' opinions, the key ingredients that would change the culture in both organizations around collaboration were trust, open communication, and mutual respect. If both management and labor exhibit mutual trust and open communication around teaching and learning, that would lead to a natural improvement in student outcomes.

There is a clear nexus between teacher quality and student achievement. The goals regarding teacher quality and student outcomes are usually jointly referred to as teaching and learning. Research on Peer Assistance Review, a teacher evaluation instrument used by some districts, all points to student achievement as an ultimate outcome. Evidence from existing literature reveals that many of the evaluation systems that are jointly developed by districts and unions use students' test scores as a measure of teacher quality and student success.

In 2011, Saul Rubinstein and his colleagues published a comprehensive report on union-management which concluded that collaboration among education stakeholders is a necessary tool for any successful, meaningful, and sustainable school reform. That sustainability is grounded in the core principles guiding the partnership between ABCUSD and the ABC Federation of Teachers (ABCFT), in which both parties committed to working together to guarantee student success and to not let each other fail. Even though each of the six school districts in the study—ABCUSD, California; Hillsborough County Public Schools, Florida; Norfolk Public School District, Virginia; Toledo School District, Ohio; Plattsburgh City School District, New York; and St. Francis Independent School District, Minnesota—was unique in its approach, the findings could be generalized due to the common patterns embedded in the experiences (Rubinstein, 2011).

In yet another study involving the ABCUSD and the ABCFT in 2014, Rubinstein found a correlation between labor-management collaboration and student achievement. His conclusions were drawn from data collected from the district's 30 schools and its more than 900 teachers. He used partnership attitude and climate surveys, data from the California Academic Performance Index (API), and social network analysis to reach those conclusions. The findings revealed that formal partnerships among administration, unions, and teachers at the school level had a significant positive impact on student performance.

The distinctive feature in the ABCUSD and the ABCFT collaborative was its targeted focus on low-performing students benefiting from free and reduced lunch and English language learning services.

The findings revealed that the collaboration was purposeful, targeted, and intentional to improve the quality of teaching and learning. The stakeholders' commitment to working together was unprecedented, especially as certain responsibilities have traditionally been those of school districts. They jointly worked to recruit, hire, compensate, and retain highly qualified teachers, as well as to improve curricular and instructional practices. The collaboration evolved over time to include textbook selection, choice of curriculum, and processes for data-based decision-making regarding student performance. The union appointed members to several committees at the district level such as the Strategic Planning Committee, the Closing the Achievement Gap Committee, and the Special Education Committee. The partnership in Norfolk was unusual because Virginia is an RTW state, but what it also revealed was that student achievement remains a common goal within union-management models (Rubinstein, 2014).

Teachers' unions, some researchers believe, have been scapegoats in education reform efforts as targeted attacks accuse them of protecting incompetent teachers and ignoring student performance. The disputes emanating from such accusations jeopardize teachers' jobs and trigger grievances against school districts. The Federal Mediation and Conciliation Services (FMCS) played an important role in arbitrating disputes between school districts and unions in the early 2000s and established a partnership that transformed the failing Charlotte County Public School District, Florida into a successful one. The involvement of the FMCS in the establishment of a labor-management council at the time is one more piece of evidence that educational partnerships lead to improved student performance. The dispute between the Charlotte County School District and the Charlotte Education Association resulted in a partnership agreement that drastically transformed a failing school system into one marked by strong student gains.

> Since 2002, the graduation rate in Charlotte County Public Schools has increased from 68% to 85% last year. Advanced Placement Test scores rose from twelfth place in Florida in 2004 to first in the state in recent results. Equally impressive, Scholastic Aptitude Test scores in reading, math, and writing for Charlotte County students have shown a 21% increase since 2004. (Cohen, 2012, p. 473)

Similar efforts in Central Falls School District, Rhode Island that were mediated by the FMCS spared 77 teachers from being dismissed and led to a labor-management agreement that planned to work on student achievement.

The push for giving teachers a voice to bring about improvements in teaching and learning has been at the forefront of unions' messaging in recent years. There is mounting evidence that partnerships between unions and school districts on student achievement can produce positive results. The Pittsburgh Public Schools and the Pittsburgh Federation of Teachers' collaboration was known to have succeeded in part because it addressed student achievement. The Promise-Ready initiative, as the collaboration was known, fostered a teaching and learning culture in every classroom for students and teachers, the focus being on keeping teachers with their students from one grade level to the next (9th grade to 10th grade, for example). In the San Juan, California Unified School district partnership, both parties used a book study, a joint Common Core committee, and a PAR initiative to foster student achievement (Spector, 2013).

Some states on the east coast of the United States have also found success with collaboration between teachers' unions and school districts. The Norfolk School District in Virginia braved state hostility toward labor unions to collaborate with its teachers' union, resulting in significant gains in student achievement (Malin, 2014). The student achievement gains earned the district the Broad Prize for Urban Education in 2005. Similar collaboration on student achievement turned around failing schools in Providence, Rhode Island, where the parties reached a deal to create a non-profit called United Providence with the goal of turning around its schools. In neighboring New Haven, Connecticut, the union and the district agreed to provide the latter flexibility in hiring, staff development, work rules, length of school day, and pedagogy in the lowest-performing schools, all with the goal of turning around those schools (Malin, 2014).

The role of school building leaders fostering collaboration to attain better student outcomes cannot be overemphasized in the discussion on school improvement. Such collaboration not only empowers teachers, but also guarantees less variability in what they teach. Under such arrangements, student performance on the state test in Union City, New Jersey increased as a result of teachers working together. The culture of the school as described by one researcher was that of a close relationship between the principal and teachers, among teachers, and between the school and families.

More collaborative relationships were conspicuously evident at the local school level in ABCUSD where principals and union building representatives met weekly on collaborative leadership teams "to discuss school issues, solve problems, and engage in site-based decision-making including textbook adoption, school schedules, and the hiring process for each school" (Rubinstein et al., 2011, p. 7). As in other collaborative initiatives, the AFT's role made a difference through the AFT Innovation Fund, which went a long way in helping with organizational learning. Site-based administrators and union leaders were trained on specific projects to enhance teaching quality and student performance. The NEA and the Gates Foundation were also supportive of collaborative organizational learning, providing $550,000 in 2012 for ongoing efforts and professional development (Anrig, 2014). There is reason to believe that institutionalized union and management collaboration between administrators and teachers around teaching and learning and other measures have largely fostered school improvement efforts.

Despite the positivity around such collaboration at the local-school level, some unions have remained skeptical of the assignment of more leadership responsibilities to their members, arguing that the focus on members' interests might erode such collaboration. In a survey distributed to 40 superintendents attending a national conference in 2009, the researcher sought to obtain the superintendents' perceptions of teacher leadership in their school districts. The findings revealed that superintendents were more willing to develop teacher leaders, but they believed that the unions acted as obstructionists to such role-sharing (Wells, 2012).

Other researchers have noted that teachers were only included in school committees to serve in subordinate roles, but not as equal partners in terms of decision-making. Coddett (2014) examined the role of building-level union leaders in collaborating with principals to effect much-needed reform and student achievement. After conducting interviews and surveying building-level union representatives working in elementary, middle, and high schools in the New York State metropolitan area, as well as reviewing school district report cards, the researcher concluded that the union leaders' role at the local school level was limited. Although teachers were included in school committees, served as mentors, and assumed other leadership roles, their roles did not amount to a full or equal partnership. Coddett (2014) noted that administrators viewed the building representatives more as advocates for teachers in conflict situations with the administration and enforcers of the contract rather than as partners.

Involving the community as allies in improving schools has had some results in districts where the effort was deliberate. Given that public schools in the United States are taxpayer funded, it would be unfair for any meaningful reform to take place without the involvement of parents. Before the COVID-19 pandemic, the active roles that parents played on boards of education demonstrated what influence they and the community at large wielded in public education. It is notable that both teachers' unions and school districts have solicited collaborative relationships far beyond just membership on school boards.

Forming alliances with parents continues to be a hallmark of teachers' unions, and the effectiveness of such alliances can be gauged only by how focused the messaging is on student welfare. It is no doubt that the success of the 2012 CTU strike was credited to the union's engagement with parents through advocacy for the non-closure of their neighborhood schools. In fact, Brogan (2016) in a review essay noted that the 2012 CTU strike was an attempt by a group of union activists to build capacity with the community using social-justice unionism to fight corporate power and austerity policies in education. In some cases, unions have used their political capital to help elect school board members who were union friendly. An example of where the union used political capital was in Plattsburgh Public School District, New York, and ABCUSD, where the union influenced school board elections by backing members who were more supportive and sympathetic to their causes. And quite obvious was the election of Brandon Johnson, a former CTU member, as mayor of Chicago in 2023.

Collaboration between unions and parents in several school districts focused on student achievement and their social-emotional wellbeing. AFT president Randi Weingarten, in an *Education Review* commentary, underscored the importance of all stakeholders—from students, to teachers, to parents, and politicians—in determining what happens in public schools. Researchers devoted time to investigating such collaboration in a study of multiple school districts. In Norfolk, Virginia, parents and community leaders were involved in the development of a Comprehensive Accountability Plan for each school, while in Toledo, Ohio, the public school district partnered with the University of Toledo to help align curricula and instructional materials used by the university with the district's specific needs. The Toledo Technology Academy received support from local businesses to provide internships and mentoring to students. In Evansville, Indiana, Malin (2014) determined that the union-management partnership led to the development of two initiatives, one of which was known as Equity Schools, which put parents and teachers together to improve student performance.

Similar to the community involvement in Toledo, the Cincinnati School District collaborated with community service providers to afford students academic, medical, and social-emotional help outside the classroom. Local social service providers were brought in to offer students medical, dental, and vision care; tutoring and mentoring support; and sports and arts programs through community learning centers. These benefits to students and their families were possible only because of the trusting relationships that existed between school administrators and the teachers' union in bringing in these outside support organizations. Services of this nature are generally provided through community schools, but in this case, the union joined forces with the school district to do what was in the best interest of students.

In the District of Columbia, the Washington Teachers' Union and management agreed in 1968 to work collaboratively to improve student achievement. In all collective bargaining agreements (CBAs) between both organizations that I reviewed from 1968 to 2019, the reasons advanced for wanting to work together included academic achievement; well-articulated programs of instruction; and shared commitment, responsibility, and accountability for student achievement. The language in the agreements calls for open communication, trust, respect, collaboration, and shared decision-making. However, Article 2.2.4 of the 2016-2019 CBA stipulates that "the school district and the teachers' union agree that matters dealing with quality education decisions are the school district's responsibility" (Washington Teachers' Union, 2019, p. 23) even though it went further to state that teachers must be allowed in the various stages of curriculum development. In spite of the contradictory language, one can still discern that there's a desire to work together toward student achievement, but the problem usually arises at the implementation phase.

Although the language in the CBA calls for collaboration in determining student outcomes, the responses from teachers that I interviewed suggest that the school district unilaterally imposes curriculum on teachers without their input. The union continues to engage the district to include its members in the development of curriculum. It is a common belief among union rank and file that some of the initiatives taken unilaterally by the school district have failed because of poor implementation and a lack of buy-in. Seeking the input of the teachers' union will lead to greater buy-in and successful implementation.

Before the COVID-19 pandemic there was a union initiative in Washington, D.C. to improve student outcomes, especially in closing the achievement gap among racial groups. The union-initiated math-literacy initiative in collaboration with the "We the People—Math Literacy for All" alliance was intended to improve student outcomes in mathematics. The alliance is a national U.S. mathematics literacy effort aimed at helping low-income students and students of color to successfully achieve mathematical skills (Algebra Project, n.d.). Through training of its members facilitated by the Young People's Project (YPP) and partnerships with other unions including the Nurses' Union, the WTU was able to sponsor students from one school to participate in one of YPP's annual math competitions called FLAGWAY. Unfortunately, with the death of former president Elizabeth Davis who established the relationship with the YPP through the math alliance, the collaboration came to an end.

Despite the acknowledgment by a teacher focus group that student achievement is a shared common vision with their administrative teams, teachers believe that the administrators do not provide opportunities to collaborate. The teachers feel the need and urgency to improve student outcomes at their respective schools but complain that the lack of collaboration impedes their abilities to attain their goals.

One teacher did, however, mention that her school was making gains in student test scores due to collaboration but cautioned that it was not enough and more needed to be done. Another teacher shared that "we care about our students, but the lack of collaboration is impacting student achievement. If they work together and truly collaborate, it will produce proficient students." While one teacher intimated that she wanted to work together with the administrative team to improve student achievement, another lamented that her attempt to collaborate with the school administration "turned into a battle instead of true collaboration." These feelings were different at another elementary school, where the teacher felt satisfied with the level of collaboration between the union and the school administration regarding student outcomes. In his view:

> When we talk about student needs, there is a lot of shared vision. We both want that students are happy and working hard and are being challenged. We agree on what students need, we agree on teaching the whole child, we agree on a rigorous curriculum. (Ngwa, 2018)

Student achievement is consistently collaborative.

From his perspective, the high student achievement in his building could partly be attributed to the collaborative relationships that existed between the school leadership team and the local union leadership team.

The opinions expressed by teacher leaders at the local school level were echoed by principals, who were asked to speak on areas where they shared a common vision with the union. One school administrator mentioned in her response to me that "I hope my vision is that which works for kids and teachers to promote teaching and learning. It seems like that is also the union's vision." She further indicated that she made decisions that were best for teachers and students within the building. That response did not make any mention of working with the teachers' union at the school to achieve those learning goals that she had stated in her first response. One school administrator reiterated the importance of increased student achievement. She added that collaboration was responsible for student achievement at her school, especially given that the school made double-digit gains in reading and math, as well as closed the achievement gap between special and general education students. She suggested that there be "a partnership between the teachers' union and management to ensure that we do what is in the best interest of children and maximize student potentials."

The sentiments of teachers and school administrators about student outcomes were the same during my field observations. At one session that was organized by the school district and attended by union leadership and members, everyone concurred that there was an achievement gap between African American students and their white counterparts, and they further agreed that the district had not adequately addressed the social-emotional needs of all children in the school system. The meeting attendees agreed to establish a shared understanding with all stakeholders around social-emotional learning competencies in the curriculum and build a culture around that. The union leadership again reiterated the collaboration between the union and the school district at another observation centered on early childhood education and social-emotional learning.

At an observation of a three-hour planning meeting, discussion took place about the union's 2018 annual shared-vison conference on math literacy for all students in the school district. Participants at the meeting included community organizations, teachers, civil rights leaders, and parents. Even though the union leader contended that the union had never been on the same page with the school district, she was satisfied that the school district was collaborating on the initiative.

At the 2018 AFT-sponsored Center for School Improvement (CSI) leadership institute, the AFT local affiliates invited all stakeholders from the school district to participate in a discussion on student achievement. Stakeholders worked collaboratively to disaggregate data on social-emotional learning, student suspensions, and the achievement gap. At the end of the three-day institute, participants from school districts agreed on the importance of working together to improve student outcomes. A four-step action plan resulted from the joint commitment that the group had developed at the end of the conference. CSI is an annual event designed to help schools improve through collaboration. Participating district teams reported success in improving their schools through the involvement of district leaders, building supervisors, teachers, and community partners.

Interviews with the hierarchy of the Washington Teachers' Union (WTU) and DC Public Schools in 2018 revealed the same goals for student achievement. The WTU president commented:

> [Teachers cannot rely] on others who are outside of our classrooms and schools to decide what works best for kids, and we've got to agree that all children, irrespective of their race, class, and gender, should have access to the best quality public education possible. That has always been my mission as a teacher: that all students are capable of learning. (Ngwa, 2018)

Another senior district official agreed with the union regarding prioritizing student outcomes, stating,

> Students are at the center of the work that we do. That's the strongest area where I'm in agreement with the teachers' union . . . When teachers feel like it's an "us versus them" mentality, that the principal is over there and we're over here, and collaboration doesn't exist, that's where you find low student achievement. (Ngwa, 2018)

Another school district leader I interviewed was more specific in describing the areas of collaboration that he would like to have with the union regarding raising student achievement. He identified closing achievement differences in the Partnership for Assessment of Readiness for College and Careers (PARCC), reducing and eliminating the large number of students scoring below grade level on state assessments, ensuring that students were performing well on the SAT and in Advanced Placement (AP) courses, making sure that more students were graduating with college credit and certifications, and making sure that "our kids are getting a great education from us working together."

The American public schools system can improve if stakeholders are intentional in their efforts to work collaboratively and in good faith to help students reach their maximum potentials. Meaningful collaboration entails everyone, irrespective of ideological differences, sitting at the table and attempting solutions for what is in the best interest of students. Teachers' unions position themselves to be part of the solution but have been tagged with negative labels to stoke public mistrust in their ability to coalesce around a good mission for kids. We can do better.

Further Reading

Algebra Project. (n.d.). Math Literacy for All. https://mathliteracyforall.org/values

Anrig, G. (2014). Cultivating collaboration: The science behind thriving labor-management relationships. *American Educator, 37*(4), 4–13.

Bangs, J., & MacBeath, J. (2012). Collective leadership: The role of teacher unions in encouraging teachers to take the lead in their own learning and in teacher policy. *Professional Development in Education, 38*(2), 331–343. doi:10.1080/19415257.2012.65

Brogan, P. (2016). Education deform and social justice unionism. *Labour/Le Travail, 77*, 225–241.

Civic Impulse. (2017a). H.R. 1—107th Congress: No Child Left Behind Act of 2001. Retrieved from https://www.govtrack.us/congress/bills/107/hr1

Civic Impulse. (2017b). H.R. 1532—112th Congress: Race to the Top Act of 2001. Retrieved from https://www.govtrack.us/congress/bills/112/hr1

Coddett, A. S. (2014). *Perceptions of the building-level union representative in principal-teacher collaboration* (Ed.D.). Fordham University, United States—New York. Retrieved from https://search-proquest-com.seu.idm.oclc.org/pqdtglobalsocsci/docview/

Cohen, G. H. (2012). Advancing student achievement in the United States public schools through labor-management collaboration: The FMCS's evolving role in education reform. *St. John's Law Review, 86*(2/3), 465–484.

Collective Bargaining Agreement, Washington Teachers' Union-District of Columbia Public School District (1968–1969).

Collective Bargaining Agreement, Washington Teachers' Union-District of Columbia Public School District (1998–2001).

Cowen, J. M., & Strunk, K. O. (2015). The impact of teachers' unions on educational outcomes: What we know and what we need to learn. *Economics of Education Review, 48*, 208–223.

Cunningham, P. (2014). An open letter to Randi Weingarten. *Education Week, 34*(11), 24–25.

Honawar, V. (2007). Accords designed to turn around troubled schools. *Education Week, 26*(41), 1-15.

Lamagna, F. G. (2010). *Factors promoting and hindering collaboration in labor-management relations.* Saybrook University, United States—California. Retrieved from https://search.proquest.com/dissertations/docview/761126867/abstract/E18D67A0F7F2403APQ/2

Lott, J., & Kenny, L. W. (2013). State teacher union strength and student achievement. *Economics of Education Review, 35*, 93–103. doi: 10.1016/j.econedurev.2013.03.006

Malin, M. H. (2014). Education reform and labor-management cooperation: What role for the law? *University of Toledo Law Review, 45*(3), 527–543.

Ngwa, T.C. (2018) *Fostering organizational change through a solutions-driven culture of collaboration. A case study of a teachers' union in the mid-Atlantic region.* ProQuest LLC.

Rubinstein, S. A. (2014). Strengthening partnerships: How communication and collaboration contribute to school improvement. *American Educator, 37*(4), 22–28.

Rubinstein, S. A., McCarthy, J. E., & Center for American Progress. (2011). *Reforming public school systems through sustained union-management collaboration.* Center for American Progress.

Rubinstein, S. A., & McCarthy, J. E. (2016). Union–management partnerships, teacher collaboration, and student performance. *ILR Review, 69*(5), 1114–1132. doi:10.1177/0019793916660508

Spector, S. (2013). Cultivating labor management collaboration. *Leadership, 42*(5), 16–19.

Washington Teachers' Union. (2025). *Collective Bargaining Agreement, 2016 - 2019.* WTU Local 6.

Wells, C. M. (2012). Superintendents' perceptions of teacher leadership in selected districts. *International Journal of Educational Leadership Preparation, 7*(2).

Weingarten, R. (2011). Voicing concerns, crafting solutions: Unions in the age of teacher bashing. *Education Review, 24*(1), 41–48.

CHAPTER 5

I Love My Job

Far and away the best prize that life has to offer is the chance to work hard at work worth doing.

— Theodore Roosevelt

Employee retention is generally determined by how much employees love and are satisfied with their jobs. The teaching profession traditionally boasted of high retention rates when teachers worked and retired at the same school or school district. These high retention rates could have been credited in part not necessarily to high compensation but to such indicators as school climate and culture, parental involvement, availability of resources, supportive teacher evaluation systems, and a generally supportive community where employees felt a sense of belonging. While teachers may genuinely love the job that they do and want to stay on, the unintended consequences of some of their working conditions would push them out prematurely. With the declining number of teachers staying in the profession, unions have stepped in to provide the support that teachers need to be successful, to feel supported at what they do, and to stay longer in the profession.

Teacher retention is important in guaranteeing staff stability and building culture in each school. Retention is a cost-saving measure on hiring and onboarding. In Washington, D.C., specifically in the traditional public school system, an average of 400 teachers are inducted each year. This number doesn't add to the existing teacher pool but rather replaces the ongoing attrition largely due to resignations and terminations. The State Board of Education estimated that in the 2019–2020 academic year alone, the school level attrition rate for District of Columbia Public Schools teachers was 17%. Although school district officials have boasted of high pay and fringe benefits for their teachers, other conditions beyond pay account for the mass exodus each year. Even the most touted high compensation, when compared to the standard of living and consumer price index in Washington, D.C., cannot afford housing and basic needs for most of the city's educators, forcing them to commute from neighboring Maryland and Virginia.

In school districts where collaboration between teachers' unions and the management is part of the culture and support is the norm, there are higher teacher retention rates and consequently higher student achievement. Some examples abound in Toledo, Ohio; Montgomery County, Maryland; and the ABC Unified School District, California.

By contrast, even though the teachers' union in D.C. and management can identify and articulate some areas of collaboration, the main area where there is a lack of collaboration—teacher evaluation—tends to be the main reason many teachers leave or are separated from the system. The D.C. teachers' union attributes the punitive nature of the teacher evaluation to be responsible for low teacher morale and the ensuing high teacher turnover from 2009 to date (Washington Teachers' Union, n.d.).

Some school leaders in the district have openly acknowledged that where there is collaboration, teachers go above and beyond what is required to fulfill the needs of the students in the school, making the teachers want to stay at the school longer. In an interview in April 2018, a high school principal attested to this notion. She associated the lack of collaboration with teacher unhappiness. As she characterized it, "an unhappy teacher makes an unhappy student" (Ngwa, 2018, p. 73). Her strategy for retaining top-quality talent in her building was to work collaboratively with the site-based union team, although that collaboration was marred by some restrictions imposed at the district level. Her strategy for retaining her teachers came down to working collaboratively with the union to identify areas where teachers were unhappy and making amends before they got to the point of leaving. Whenever she heard that her teachers could potentially leave because of something or conditions they were unhappy about, she consulted the union representative to make sure that the issue was resolved using her School Chapter Advisory (SCAC) team, a team constituted of mostly union members meeting with the principal and, in some cases, with members of the administrative team. Through an open-door policy, consultation with the SCAC team, and constantly listening to teachers, she was able to retain more teachers than were other schools.

Another D.C. principal I spoke with believed that because teachers felt ownership in the school and could identify with its successes, they were willing to work and retire from there. She further intimated that in addition to collaborating with the administration to improve all aspects of the school, some teachers felt a sense of belonging because of the community ties they had with the school. In such cases, the teachers returned to teach at the same schools they attended and eventually enrolled their children there. In addition to the sense of community and belonging, the union-negotiated contract intentionally created avenues for collaboration among the administration, the teachers, and parents and community members. Such intentional collaboration among stakeholders, when judiciously and appropriately implemented, served as an impetus for teachers to stay longer at the school.

The former president of the Washington Teachers' Union, Elizabeth Davis, concluded that "naturally, if teachers are happy in their schools, they are going to stay; if they are not, they want to leave" (Ngwa, 2018, p. 74). She added that collaboration would only be effective between local school leaders and teachers if the hierarchy of the union and management modeled the collaboration. She stressed that school climate was an important indicator of teacher retention and "when teachers feel respected and they are integral parts of the school community, they stay" Ngwa, 2018, p. 74).

Shortly after taking over as chancellor of D.C. Public Schools, Antwan Wilson sought to establish positive relationships with the union as a way of rebuilding the damage caused to teacher morale by his predecessors Michelle Rhee and Kaya Henderson through their hard-handed leadership styles. During his short-lived tenure, he attended union events, interacted with teachers, and generally was of the opinion that teachers would stay at a school longer so long as they felt ownership in the school and believed that they could call it home.

School Improvement and Teacher Retention

There is a correlation between labor-management collaboration and school improvement, as espoused by a member of the WTU who participated in a focus group that I hosted back in 2018. The lack of collaboration, she said, affects teacher morale and school improvement. That sentiment was echoed by her colleague who attributed her school falling short on school improvement to the lack of collaboration. Another teacher from a separate school argued that there was no way of measuring the impact of collaboration on anything in her school due to the lack of such cooperation. She hoped that forming a unified collective front to present issues to the principal, as opposed to her as the building representative, might put pressure on the school leader to be open to collaboration, which could probably improve their school culture. She added that the administrative team had difficulty retaining teachers because of the toxic school culture, which resulted in her colleagues feeling a sense of disillusionment and leaving. Separately, another teacher added that the lack of collaboration resulted in low teacher morale and an ensuing drop in student achievement at her school. She pointed out that a lot of older and more experienced teachers had either left or had been pushed out because of the frustration from the administration refusing to engage with them meaningfully about their diverse grievances. Similarly, some teachers described their buildings as toxic and sick, yet the principal was oblivious to it, and they feared collaboration with the union because they wanted to maintain a culture of oppression. These teachers hoped that using the union to help them collaborate with the administration could pave the way for the school to be a pleasant place for adults and students. For one teacher, collaboration made people go above and beyond to fulfill the needs of the school, making teachers want to stay at the school longer. She further explained,

> It makes people go above and beyond to fulfill the needs of the school; it leads to greater retention, mainly because you can problem-solve before it becomes a problem, people getting burned out, getting upset, or getting in trouble. A lot of times administration forgets how much time something that sounds small and easy can take, and if they don't talk to us first, maybe they don't realize that something is putting a huge burden and stress on people, and that can cause people to look elsewhere. So, I think the more that everyone can work together to meet the goals and initiatives of the district and to work with our kids, then, the better the school runs. (Ngwa, 2018, p. 72)

These sentiments were corroborated by some school leaders who associated the lack of collaboration with unhappiness. Another school principal contended that it was impossible to improve a school without collaborating with teachers and their union. She expressed that thought in the following statement:

> I believe that it's impossible to improve a school without collaborating with teachers because teachers must have the buy-in, and as the leader of the building, you may not know what exactly teachers need, and if you don't have their input, you may make the wrong decisions as it leads to improvement efforts. So, I do believe in collaborating with teachers and their union. I think that that has an impact on just the high retention that I have in my school. (Ngwa, 2018, p. 73)

Both teachers and school leaders agree and understand that naturally, if teachers are happy in their schools, they are going to stay; if they are not, they want to leave. What the union leadership has pushed for many years is effective collaboration at the local school level between their members and their school leaders while forging theirs with central office administrators, notably not only with the chancellor, but also with the mayor's office, instructional superintendents, and the lawyers at the Labor Management and Employee Relations (LMER) office. Schools can't improve absent teacher satisfaction and retention; school improvement is a recipe for student achievement.

Collaborative Partnerships

For as long as the WTU has entered into collaborative bargaining agreements (CBAs) with the school district, it has made a concerted effort to include an article on collaborative partnerships. Including an article which they termed *Full and Equal Partnership* (FEP) was their way of creating an avenue for the union and management to make decisions collaboratively. The article encouraged collaboration between the chancellor and the union president and between principals and building representatives. The long-term goal for such partnerships is to improve teacher satisfaction, which would likely translate into high retention rates, and ultimately improve student outcomes. Some of their CBAs have included a memorandum of agreement which established the District Collaborative: Supporting Teaching and Academic Reform (DCSTAR) with the mission of enhancing stakeholder collaboration, a collaborative decision-making panel around an extended school year, and the best form of schools for each community.

Some of the existing collaborative initiatives that I observed during my data collection process aligned with the structures established by the CBAs. For example, at one school, the SCAC was observed working collaboratively on grading issues and other initiatives. During the meeting that was led by the building union representative, the members pledged to work together on the grading issue and were planning a follow-up meeting in the interim to continue working on the same problem.

During my tenure as a union leader at the local school level and as executive director, I participated in meetings that involved members of the public schools leadership team, the leadership team of the union, teachers, principals, and parents. One such meeting was a debriefing of the Public Education Leadership Project (PELP) summer institute that the school's chancellor and some members of his team attended together with union leaders and school administrators. The collaborative initiative they addressed at the meeting focused on the Social-Emotional and Academic Development (SEAD) framework that the district was adopting to help with the social-emotional needs of students. Stakeholders at the session committed to building a shared understanding of social-emotional learning competencies in the schools' curriculum. These are the type of initiatives that the union and teachers have championed over the years to ensure that their members felt heard, seen, and respected and expressed a love for their jobs.

The annual AFT-sponsored Center for School Improvement (CSI) leadership conference which is held at the United Federation of Teachers headquarters in New York is an all-inclusive collaborative initiative. Participants from the conference are local school teams invited by the teachers' union and include stakeholders from the union, members of the district management team, parents, members of State Boards of Education, school administrators, and teachers. The WTU has consistently participated at this conference, intentionally alternating members from local school teams as a way of building cohesion at the local school level. Initiatives of this nature that bring in teachers to work with members of their school community have the long-lasting effect of boosting morale and helping with retention.

Local School Climate and Culture

The stories of teachers working together at their local school communities have all yielded positive results especially in the area of teacher satisfaction. In cases where teachers have expressed a lack of collaboration with their school administrators, there has been a lot of frustration, but in cases where they have worked together, the outcomes have been beneficial to the entire school community, and the energy among faculty has been high. At a local school where the union building representative pressured the administrative team to work together with the teachers on the master schedule, the results inspired the school leader to want to collaborate even more over the summer in preparation for the next school year by allocating additional resources in teacher stipends for their time. At another school, teachers expressed excitement at having worked with the leadership team on the transportation plan, the school's extended hours, and the Science, Technology, Engineering, the Arts, and Mathematics (STEAM) initiative for the school. In spite of the structures embedded in the CBA to help with collaboration, the refusal by some school leaders to collaborate with their teachers has led to severe sentiments of frustration. The union's message to its members has consistently been to refrain from the culture of complaining but to seek solutions through collaboration and common ground, yet the culture of unilateral and top-down decision-making at some schools has demoralized and forced teachers to leave either the school or the profession entirely.

The school leaders I spoke to did not have much to share about what they did collectively with the union teams at their schools in the past. While one school leader expressed an interest in collaborating on the use of paper and the master schedule for the next school year, she did not genuinely see any areas where she thought she could use shared leadership as a way of accomplishing the school's goals. As a new school leader, she hoped as she grew in the profession, she would feel more comfortable collaborating with her teachers and their union representatives.

School leaders who have attended joint trainings or conferences with their union leaders and invested in professional development for their teachers have seen an improvement in school culture. Constant communication, a shared commitment to closing the achievement gap, and collaboratively identifying initiatives that would benefit the school community would encourage teachers to want to work at a school. This has been validated by school leaders who previously participated at the union's shared vision conference and had open lines of communication between their leadership teams and their teachers.

Relationships

Building relationships served as a catalyst to the collaboration that occurred between members of the union and the school district at all levels. When educators build trust and transparency, and establish mutual respect, there is no doubt they will want to share the same workspace for many years to come. What "Teacher 6" in my focus group had to share was compelling and depicted a very positive image of the relationships between her principal and members of the union. She expressed her thoughts in the following statements: "We can come to her with open dialogue." "We keep the lines of communication open." "He's [the principal] very open to having union events." "They [the administration] are open to people taking leadership roles." "They're pretty open to feedback." The most telling comment was that "[the principal is known for] always having a very open door policy" (Ngwa, 2018, p. 81).

The school leaders who build cordial professional relationships with building union representatives and field services specialists see the difference in the positive responses from their teachers to requests that, in some cases, do not fall within the scope of the CBA. One principal that I interviewed described her relationship with the union as strong, but, most especially, the relationship with the entire staff at her school was collegial. She described it in these words:

> But just the relationship that I have with teachers in the building overall, a lot of the stuff really doesn't go to the level where you really have to use the contract, because we have shared leadership, just open-door policies where teachers are able to voice their concerns and express how they feel. (Ngwa, 2018, p. 82)

When DC Public Schools' local leaders fail to establish positive relationships with the teachers in their buildings, the following frustrations are commonplace: "She doesn't see that it comes from the top when you berate people in public." "You call yourself collaborating, but you collaborate with the people that would be your 'yes' people instead of the ones that are going to challenge you." "Certain teachers are treated differently than other teachers, especially our senior teachers." "She's not seen, she's not visible."

A participant from the school district and a member of the union leadership team echoed the same thoughts on relationships. For District Leader 2, "where you see collaboration, you see trust in the relationship." He added that "people and teachers need to feel respected, and I agree with them. Respect isn't too much to ask for." His counterpart in the union mirrored the same opinion:

> If the administration respected their teaching force, teachers would respect each other. You would actually have students that would

> step up and would respect teachers and administrators. Once you have respect for each other and what each one's role is, then you can actually work together. (Ngwa, 2018, p. 82)

She underscored that the respectful relationships that the union developed with the school district were important in determining how much respect both entities received from policymakers, the council members, and the mayor and her deputy. Her close collaborator, Union Leader 2, attributed the success they had with professional development courses to the relationships that they established with school principals or administrators.

The importance of workplace climate to employee retention cannot be overemphasized. Teachers have traditionally earned the respect of the communities in which they work and, in some cases, have received perks from vendors in appreciation of their services. Although Congress didn't proclaim National Teacher Appreciation Day until 1980, teachers have generally been appreciated in many ways and, in return, have served their school communities longer, in spite of insufficient compensation. The pressures imposed on the profession by policy-makers through unreasonable accountability measures in the form of standardized assessments, school rankings (report cards), and merit-based evaluation systems, coupled with top-down decision-making, have diminished morale and forced many to resign or retire early. The support mechanisms put in place by teachers' unions, if welcome and supported by school districts, would reignite the pride and love that many had for the profession.

Further Reading

Collective Bargaining Agreement, Washington Teachers' Union-District of Columbia Public School District (1968–1969).

Collective Bargaining Agreement, Washington Teachers' Union-District of Columbia Public School District (1998–2001).

Collective Bargaining Agreement, Washington Teachers' Union-District of Columbia Public School District (2016–2019).

District of Columbia Office of the State Superintendent of Education (2024): School Report Card Accountability Scores. https://osse.dc.gov/page/dc-school-report-card-resource-library

District of Columbia State Board of Education (2021): Teacher and Principal Attrition in the District's Public Schools. https://sboe.dc.gov/

Ngwa, T.C. (2018). *Fostering organizational change through a solutions-driven culture of collaboration. A case study of a teachers' union in the mid-Atlantic region*. ProQuest LLC.

Roosevelt, T. (1916). *The key to success in life*. Federated Publishing.

Rubinstein, S. A. (2014). Strengthening partnerships: How communication and collaboration contribute to school improvement. *American Educator, 37*(4), 22–28.

Rubinstein, S. A., & McCarthy, J. E. (2016). Union–management partnerships, teacher collaboration, and student performance. *ILR Review, 69*(5), 1114–1132.

Rubinstein, S. A., McCarthy, J. E., & Center for American Progress. (2011). *Reforming public school systems through sustained union-management collaboration*. Center for American Progress.

WTU Local 6. (n.d.). *IMPACT petition*. https://www.wtulocal6.net/impact_petition

CHAPTER 6

The Power of Negotiations

Our experience has taught us that with goodwill a negotiated solution can be found for even the most profound problems.

— Nelson Mandela

The National Labor Relations Act of 1935 laid the groundwork that protects workers' unrestricted right to association. The law further protects workers at the workplace, regardless of whether or not they are unionized. The right of employees to bargain collectively is enshrined in the National Labor Relations Board (NLRB) which is the deferral statute that grants private sector employees the right to join a union and negotiate their working conditions with their respective employers. Local and State government employees however do not automatically benefit from this statute, except if their legislatures expressly grant such rights or if there is an executive order to that effect. States that have passed laws that restrict collective bargaining are referred to as Right to Work States. Under collective bargaining agreements (CBAs), employees and employers can negotiate compensation, working conditions, and benefits.

A new era in collective bargaining came about as a result of national unions advocating for a different type of unionism, *new unionism* or *solutions-driven unionism* (Eberts, 2007), as an alternative to the social-movement unionism of the 1960s and 1970s that was more radical and adversarial. Today there is general agreement in the education community, including among union leadership, that the conversation needs to revolve around student achievement first and foremost. Progressive union leaders are constantly pushing for teachers' voices to be part of the reform process. Collective bargaining agreements therefore would appear incomplete without the explicit inclusion of collaboration on teacher quality and student achievement.

Collaborative collective bargaining gives teachers a voice in decision-making. Randi Weingarten, the AFT president, sees collective-bargaining collaboration as a means of enhancing the teaching profession, uplifting foundational strategies and solutions in teaching and learning all over. In at least four school districts, collaborative structures have been set up around collective bargaining. Noggle (2009) found that there was consensus among labor and management that collaboration was important to their next collective bargaining talks, especially around teacher quality and student achievement, as well as for the improvement of labor-management relations. Koza (2009) revealed that there was a positive relationship between collective bargaining items such as instructional/pupil contact time, length of the school day, and to an extent, allocated in-service days. Negotiated increased instructional time and a longer school day were associated with higher student achievement, as evidenced by student test scores.

Per these researchers, districts that embraced the collaborative bargaining approach tended to spend less time on their collective bargaining negotiations. In the few school districts where the collective bargaining process evolved beyond teachers' economic interests, job security, and due process rights, collective bargaining was an ongoing process.

In a collaborative collective bargaining process, both sides typically ignore the notion of scoring wins for themselves and their constituents; instead, winning is mutual, and both sides are willing to make concessions. That's the power of win-win collective bargaining. In 2017, both the union president and the chancellor of the D.C. Public Schools system agreed that interest-based collective bargaining was best for schools and students. The chancellor agreed that teachers were not unreasonable to demand a new contract. For him, collaborating with the union in the collective bargaining process was another way of respecting the work that teachers do. Consequently, he gave more attention to negotiations over an expired contract between the union and DCPS than his predecessor did, and eventually ratified the said contract in August 2017. Unlike his predecessor,

Kaya Henderson, Antwan Wilson, the chancellor who precipitated the negotiation of this collective bargaining agreement, believed that negotiating an agreement with teachers was a priority that required a win-win approach rather than each side positioning itself to win while the other loses. He understood that being able to reach an agreement with teachers on their contract would send a message that he respected them and the work that they did with students.

> Feeling like a deal can be reached in terms of pay when the improvements are happening. . . . We are improving as a school district. The people who are helping drive that improvement spend a lot of time in classrooms with kids, and so it can be both ways. It can't be that we have improvements, but we can't have a deal done in five years. If we have improvement, we need those people in classrooms so that we are great. We have the next five years and we need to do even more. I can't have them thinking that we're asking them to lose. (Ngwa, 2018, pp. 66-67)

Although his tenure was short-lived due to a controversy over his daughter's school placement, he certainly gained the respect of teachers and their union with respect to the collective bargaining agreement and especially the long-anticipated pay raise that did not occur under the previous chancellor.

Bargaining under Antwan Wilson's successor looked very different, although not as difficult as under Michelle Rhee and Kaya Henderson. Although the union notified the new chancellor Lewis Ferebee at the expiration of the collective bargaining agreement of its intent to begin negotiations, it took several follow-up emails before the two teams began meeting to establish ground rules.

The establishment of ground rules in my opinion is the most collaborative phase of the collective bargaining process. Parties tend to be more flexible and generally refrain from taking hardline positions that would stall the process. Shortly after the commencement of the process, the chief negotiator for the school district resigned from her position and was succeeded by a more collaborative individual, who not only understood labor more than did her predecessor, but was a former employee of the union. That relationship, however, in no way gave the union any unfair advantage, but was helpful in ushering in a general sense of understanding that was not present previously. The collaboration was, however, short-lived because unlike the union negotiating team, the chief negotiator for DCPS was not necessarily the decision-maker. In an education system that is run by the mayor, otherwise known as *mayoral control*, there are several layers of decision-making, with the final say resting in the hands of the mayor. Without the school's chancellor actively negotiating, the process tends to be slow, as decisions need to follow a chain of command.

Multiple factors contributed to the delay in reaching agreement over the collective bargaining agreement that expired in September 2019. First, the COVID-19 pandemic shifted the attention of the negotiators to bargaining over health and wellness conditions for educators and their students before the reopening of schools; second, the sudden death of the chief negotiator for the union in a car accident and the eventual transition and restructuring of the union's team contributed to the delay; finally, the inability of the parties to reach agreement over compensation resulted in an impasse which was referred to the Public Employees Relation Board (PERB) for mediation. In spite of the procedural challenges, the union was able to leverage its community partnerships through engagement in a contract campaign to pressure the school system and the mayor to close out the contract. In addition to the pay raises included in the current contract, the parties also signed MOAs on a Climate Curriculum Taskforce to develop curriculum that infuses climate literacy in schools and on Diversity of Instructional Staff which focuses on the recruitment of teachers of color.

The COVID-19 Pandemic

Negotiations took a different turn when in the spring of 2020 the world order was disrupted by a global pandemic. On March 11, 2020 the World Health Organization declared the novel coronavirus, COVID-19, that was first detected in Wuhan, China in late winter, a global pandemic. While the mayor of Washington D.C. declared a state of emergency and businesses/organizations either shut down or transitioned to remote work, schools also closed their doors and resorted to virtual learning. This transition had major ramifications for contract negotiations between the two parties who had hitherto met weekly, alternating between their respective headquarters.

When parties commit to engage in collective bargaining, the understanding is that they will negotiate in good faith. In the District of Columbia, the collective bargaining statute is regulated by the Public Employees Relations Board (PERB). The PERB certifies and decertifies labor organizations, adjudicates unfair labor complaints, determines whether a particular subject is within the scope of bargaining, and facilitates the resolution of impasses in contract negotiations, among other responsibilities (Public Employee Relations Board, n.d.). This body became very instrumental in resolving major differences between the two parties as the COVID-19 pandemic unfolded.

Although the CBA that expired in September 2019 remained in effect throughout negotiations, many of the provisions needed to be modified to adapt to the status quo which was the virtual environment in which almost all organizations operated. The instrument that is used under these circumstances is either a Memorandum of Understanding or a Memorandum of Agreement which both parties exploited to the maximum.

Both parties initially agreed to hold contract negotiations virtually, but before that occurred, they also thought they could reach agreement on lower-level grievances. Even though there was a verbal agreement between the Labor Management and Employee Relations (LMER) team and the union, the latter thought it was best having a written agreement that they each could adhere to. Surprisingly, when the union submitted a draft of the agreement for review and eventual signature, LMER returned with an expansion of the hearings to include higher-level cases, some of which required the services of an independent arbitrator. The failure of both teams to agree to this expansion caused the school district to renege on its previous commitment to conduct collective bargaining sessions virtually. For lack of options, the union filed an Unfair Labor Practice (ULP) complaint with the PERB to help resolve the deadlock between the two parties. This ULP would constitute one of several complaints that the union filed in the summer and the fall of 2020.

As is customary with the PERB, the body assigned a mediator to try to get the parties to an agreement. Being cognizant of the challenges posed by the COVID-19 pandemic and the backlogs that not conducting some hearings would cause, the union agreed to poll its members to determine how many of them with active grievances would agree to participating in virtual hearings via a video platform. Even though a substantial number of the grievants responded in the affirmative, many for good reason refused, preferring to wait until after life returned to normal in order to have their day in front of a hearing officer or an arbitrator. The union and its lawyers argued that allowing any arbitration hearings to proceed virtually would put its members at a disadvantage, given that arbitration is usually the last step of the grievance process without any opportunity to appeal. That argument still did not deter the school district from adding language to the mediation settlement that would have penalized individuals who turned down an opportunity for a virtual hearing. This created a deadlock in mediation that caused the two organizations to return to the arbitrator for a full hearing that was ruled in favor of the WTU. DCPS was ordered to cease and desist from attempting to circumvent the WTU by dealing directly with employees represented by the latter and to negotiate in good faith moving forward.

Events took a dramatic turn when DCPS started planning a student return to in-person learning in the fall of 2020. Virtual instruction had been successful to a certain extent in the spring after the city's mayor declared a state of emergency and schools closed on March 13. Students in the affluent parts of the city benefitted more because of their access to technology and their parents' privilege to work from home and support them. This however was not the case in the poorer parts of the city where access to technology was a problem and where most parents did not have white collar jobs that afforded them the opportunity to work remotely. It was, as has always been the case in the District of Columbia, a tale of two cities in one. The WTU joined forces with allies to demand digital equity for all students, as there were still students without computers or those with computers but no connectivity to the Internet. The mounting pressure put district education leaders and the mayor's office on the defensive and under pressure, yet learning gaps remained, absenteeism remained a problem in certain parts of the city, and teachers were left frustrated that even the students who showed up for classes were not turning in work.

Virtual learning clearly was not working in the District of Columbia Public Schools, widening an already existing academic achievement gap. Everyone agreed that there was no replacement for in-person learning, but rather than bringing all stakeholders to the table to find the safest solution to returning to in-person learning, the schools' chancellor and the mayor preferred a top-down approach that infuriated teachers, administrators, and parents. Teachers and other educators were sidelined as the city's mayor appointed an advisory group to advise her on reopening the city and the schools. Although the WTU president eventually insisted on being included in the advisory group, her opinions were not representative of those of her members.

In an attempt to use the collective bargaining process as a tool to force the school district to collaborate, the union put together a taskforce to develop recommendations that could guide the schools to safely reopen. The taskforce of over 200 educators included teachers, librarians, general education and special education teachers. The taskforce's report was guided and aligned with a plan that the AFT released earlier in the spring entitled, "Plan to Safely Reopen America's Schools and Communities" which served as a guide to its locals. The five pillars that served as a guide to the AFT plan included:

1. Maintaining physical distancing until the number of new cases declines for at least 14 consecutive days.
2. Putting in place the infrastructure and resources to test, trace, and isolate new cases.
3. Deploying the public health tools that prevent the virus' spread and aligning them with education strategies that meet the needs of students.
4. Involving workers, unions, parents, and communities in all planning.
5. Investing in recovery: Do not abandon America's communities or forfeit America's future (American Federation of Teachers, 2020).

The set of recommendations sought to ensure the safety of educators and students as the district considered gradually returning them to in-person learning in the fall. They also called for increased investment of $11 million to ensure that each student received a computer or tablet for the upcoming school year. The report was submitted to the city's leaders on June 22, 2020, and briefings were scheduled to share key highlights and answer questions. Although council members who have an oversight duty over education were open to the recommendations, the chancellor's and the mayor's offices seemed to have less appetite for any sort of collaboration invoking management rights over bargaining. The parties would however return to the bargaining table to negotiate a Memorandum of Agreement (MOA) on reopening schools after the PERB ruled in favor of the teachers' union in an Unfair Labor Practice (ULP) complaint. Even though weekly negotiations were taking place, DCPS was actively attempting to make unilateral decisions with respect to reopening schools, and proceeded to send guidelines for return to in-person work and a survey to teachers in June 2021 called the *Intent to Return* form. The survey sought to capture the number of teachers who intended to return to in-person teaching when schools reopened but also came with a penalty for not filling it out. Outraged by how DCPS was moving forward without collaborating or bargaining, the union took multiple actions to challenge them. The union president asked her members not to complete the survey and made a formal bargaining demand and a set of information requests regarding the *Intent to Return* form to the schools' chancellor. She also filed a class grievance over the issue and a complaint and preliminary injunction motion with the D.C. PERB. As a result of those actions, DCPS later informed WTU that its members would not be disciplined for not completing the *Intent to Return* form.

In the meantime, the COVID-19 pandemic was raging. The number of infections was increasing both locally and nationwide, and the number of deaths soared. The future was uncertain for everyone, and anxiety and trepidation gripped the nation. There was uncertainty in the education community, and health experts projected a gloomy outlook especially leading into the winter months. While some school districts took proactive measures and made plans for virtual learning through the first quarter of the 2020–2021 school year, DC Public Schools continued to make plans for in-person learning for August. In private, even central office staff were not at ease with the plans that were driven in most part by politicians in the mayor's office. Teachers and other educators found it difficult to understand how schools could reopen when the city was still under a state of emergency that was declared in March and the health department's metrics for reopening the city as a whole had not been met. The only logical conclusion was that decisions were driven by politics rather than science.

The Role of the Public Employee Relations Board

The District of Columbia Public Employee Relations Board (PERB) is the referee in ongoing boxing matches between employers and labor unions in the city. Its role is to ensure that there are no knock-out punches to any party, but that there is fairness in how both management and labor treat each other in their day-to-day relations. It is the reason why mediation is always an option that allows parties to reach a win-win solution. Among other responsibilities, the Board seeks to adjudicate unfair labor practice complaints, determines whether a particular subject or proposal is within the scope of bargaining, and facilitates the resolution of impasses in contract negotiations (Public Employee Relations Board, n.d.).

Over of the summer and throughout the fall of 2020, the number of complaints that were filed by the WTU increased significantly as a result of actions taken by DCPS during the COVID-19 pandemic. During this period, the PERB took some actions that were unprecedented, which I can only assume were influenced by their desire to curb the anxiety that everyone was experiencing from the pandemic. Complaints that typically took a considerable amount of time to be ruled on were fast-tracked and, in several cases, decisions were rendered without checking for any dissent. It is worth noting that the five-member board is appointed by the mayor with the advice and consent of the D.C. Council. These five members include a chair, a labor member, two public members, and a management member. The assumption among the common citizen is that because the members are appointed by the mayor, somehow they owe allegiance to the city's agencies, but it is fair to give credit to Board members for their impartiality especially with respect to previous and ongoing labor disputes between DCPS and the WTU. From the start of the COVID-19 pandemic through December of that year, the WTU filed a total of four Unfair Labor Practice complaints with the PERB and prevailed in all of them. When the union failed to sign the Return to In-Person Memorandum of Agreement (MOA) that it had negotiated with the school district, the latter, in response, turned to the PERB for remedy, but a last-minute agreement before the Christmas break also led the District to agree to withdrawing the complaint within seven days.

PERB decisions have a way of putting the losing party in an awkward position—one that tends to create the semblance of humiliation. Under normal circumstances, when the PERB rules on a matter, there is an added clause at the end that the losing party must post the notice at a location that is visible to all members of the union's bargaining unit for 30 days. During the COVID-19 pandemic, members of the union became accustomed to emails from DCPS Communications that stated in part that "we will negotiate in good faith with WTU, upon request."

Seeking common ground remains the most viable way for teachers' unions and their members' employers to navigate otherwise complex situations. Where negotiations have deadlocked, using mediation and other legal instruments to help the parties return to the bargaining table serves their purposes. After all, if both parties truly agree that they care about children and their success, they have a responsibility to negotiate in good faith to avoid causing any collateral damage to the families that rely on them.

Further Reading

American Federation of Teachers. (2020). *A plan to safely reopen America's schools and communities: Guidance for imagining a new normal for public education, public health and our economy in the age of COVID-19.* https://www.aft.org/sites/default/files/media/2020/covid19_reopen-america-schools.pdf

Collective Bargaining Agreement, Washington Teachers' Union-District of Columbia Public Schools, 2020–2023.

Eberts, R. W. (2007). Teachers unions and student performance: Help or hindrance? *Future of Children, 17*(1), 175–200.

Koza, P. L. (2009). *New Jersey teacher negotiated contracts items and their relationship to student achievement.* Widener University, United States—Pennsylvania. Retrieved from https://search.proquest.com/dissertations/docview/305137117/abstract/

Mandela, N. (1994). *Long walk to freedom: The autobiography of Nelson Mandela.* Little, Brown and Company.

Ngwa, T.C. (2018) *Fostering organizational change through a solutions-driven culture of collaboration. A case study of a teachers' union in the mid-Atlantic region.* ProQuest LLC.

Noggle, M. K. (2009). *Win-win: A case study of collaborative structures between labor and management.* Temple University, United States—Pennsylvania. Retrieved from https://search.proquest.com/docview/305016065/abstract/2C5A4F7D4B9B4E26PQ/1

Public Employee Relations Board. (n.d.). *PERB responsibilities.* DC.gov. https://perb.dc.gov/page/perb-responsibilities

Sustar, L. (2013). Teachers' unions at the crossroads: Can the assault on teachers be rebuffed? *New Labor Forum (Sage Publications Inc.), 22*(2), 60–68. doi:10.1177/10957960134832

U.S. Congress. *(1934) United States Code: National Labor Relations, 29 U.S.C. §§ 151–166 Suppl. 2.* [Periodical] https://www.loc.gov/item/uscode1934-003029007/

Washington Teachers' Union v. District of Columbia Public Schools (PERB Case No. 24-N-04), (April 04, 2024), D.C. Reg.72(2025)

Weingarten, R. (2011). Voicing concerns, crafting solutions: Unions in the age of teacher bashing. *Education Review, 24*(1), 41–48.

CHAPTER 7

Political Influence

We care. We fight. We show up. We vote. AND WE SAVE LIVES AND OUR DEMOCRACY.

— American Federation of Teachers

The strength of unions resides in their ability to effectively organize rather than simply provide services to their members. This organizing model is built on the notion that there is more strength in numbers, and unions have used that to their advantage to build power. The rallying call for organizing is also rooted in the ideals of democracy. It is based on the notion that when individuals collectively organize in a democracy, they can leverage that to hold elected officials accountable, especially in supporting their workplace conditions. While wealthy donors influence elections through heavy financial contributions, organized labor uses its numbers to influence elections, legislative processes, and policies. In recent years, especially with the advent of an unfriendly political majority in Washington and rightwing states, the two largest teachers' unions have used these numbers as leverage for their agendas. Not only have the unions taken an active role in shaping policy, but also, they have educated, encouraged, and supported their members to run for political office. There has been a steady rise in the number of teachers running for seats on local and state boards of education as well as state and national legislatures with the backing of their colleagues. With over 1.8 million members at the American Federation of Teachers and over 3.2 million at the National Education Association, even with the attempted weakening of unions' power through the landmark Supreme Court ruling in *Janus v. AFSCME* in June 2018, both organizations remain a political force to reckon with.

Election of Teachers to Office

Historically, many teachers have not sought political office, especially at the national level. However, a few politicians in history have sought the role including First Lady Eleanor Roosevelt and President Lyndon Johnson, who ran and won a campaign for the highest office in the country.

The changing landscape of education and threats to teachers' power, membership, and influence have motivated a voting block—one that has traditionally been interested in the respect for their profession and improving both their working conditions and the learning conditions of their students—to play a direct role in shaping education policy. In addition to existing threats to union members, the gutting of public unions by the 2018 *Janus v. AFSCME* Supreme Court decision created an opening and an urgency for teachers to run for local and national elected office.

In Connecticut, Jahana Hayes, who came into the spotlight after being honored as National Teacher of the Year in 2016 by President Barack Obama, won the congressional seat in 2018. She joined her neighbor, Massachusetts senator Elizabeth Warren—who has called teaching her "first love" and has constantly spoken out against attacks on public school teachers—as one of the few teachers on Capitol Hill in addition to Mark Takano who was elected to represent California's 39th district in 2012. Tim Walz, a former high school social studies teacher and football coach who was elected to Minnesota's 1st congressional district in 2006, was elected as his state's governor in 2018, was reelected in 2022, and was tapped to serve as Kamala Harris's running mate in the 2024 presidential election.

In Chicago politics, it is no secret that the CTU has brought down powerful mayors such as Lightfoot, the one-term mayor who took on the union during the 2019 strike and over school reopenings during the pandemic, Rham Emmanuel, as well as other influential public officials including council members and county commissioners. In addition to electing union-friendly candidates to fill some of these roles, the union took a bold step in 2023 to propel its former member Brandon Johnson to the mayoral seat in an election that sent shockwaves through the city.

Quite naturally, these teachers or former teachers could not have been elected to political office without the support of teachers' unions and their members. Electing one of theirs puts them in a position of strength and guarantees that their issues will be prioritized.

Local and National Elections

Every candidate who runs for office understands the significance of an endorsement from groups that wield a massive following like teachers' unions. It is no surprise then that candidates running for local and national office have solicited endorsements from these two influential unions and their locals.

During the 2020 Democratic primaries, with an extremely crowded field of candidates running, the AFT took a different approach to candidate endorsements. The organization organized townhalls in various cities where the candidates made their case to members on why they were the best deserving of their endorsements. These townhalls were unique opportunities for the candidates to explain not only their educational plans and the benefit to students, but also how much support they would provide to unions once in office. One could tell from comments that members posted on social media what their leanings were. Elizabeth Warren as a former teacher was appealing to many teachers, especially as she constantly touted her support for unions. Bernie Sanders with a massive following among young people also bragged about his support for unions and courted the major teachers' unions for endorsement. Joe Biden touted his deep roots and ties in Scranton, Pennsylvania where he grew up and constantly referenced his wife who is a teacher. The slogan "We care. We fight. We show up. We vote. AND WE SAVE LIVES AND OUR DEMOCRACY" became a rallying call for AFT members to demonstrate how influential they are in the political process and in holding elected officials accountable. Members display the slogan on t-shirts, head bandanas, and other apparel as a reminder of how powerful their voices can be in a democracy.

American Federation of Teachers Slogan

From Detroit, Michigan with then-Senator Kamala Harris to Philadelphia, PA with Senator Elizabeth Warren; Lordstown, OH with Senator Bernie Sanders; Albany, NY with Rep. Tim Ryan; Yonkers, NY with Senator Amy Klobuchar; Las Vegas, NV with Julian Castro; Washington, D.C. with Gov. Steve Bullock; Houston, TX with Vice President Joe Biden; Miami, FL with Beto O'Rourke; and culminating with a Public Education Forum in Pittsburgh, PA, members challenged the candidates to commit to supporting public education and defending the values for which they stand.

While the AFT did not formally take a position to endorse any specific candidate, it did allow locals the flexibility to endorse one of three candidates late into the primaries season: Senator Elizabeth Warren, who was endorsed by the Boston Teachers' Union; Senator Bernie Sanders, endorsed by AFT Vermont; and Vice President Biden, endorsed by the Scranton Federation of Teachers.

Prior to the union leaders' town hall meeting at which Randi Weingarten announced the decision of the executive council not to endorse any particular candidate, the Washington Teachers' Union (WTU) had already endorsed Senator Bernie Sanders using its local process of endorsing candidates for office through member engagement, an endorsement recommendation to the executive board by the Committee on Political Education (COPE), and an eventual vote by the representative assembly. In a political climate where young people were more energized than ever, it came as no surprise that the WTU would endorse Sanders, who happened to be the preferred candidate of many young people, and understandably so because of his progressive positions and support for public education. Not only was the WTU's COPE chaired by an energic young member, but also many of the committee's members were millennials and preferred Sanders.

In the lead-up to the democratic presidential primaries, the WTU had distinguished itself among the other unions in the D.C. metro area by becoming very politically active. Local candidates for city council, the State Board of Education (SBOE), and even the mayor, who had no clear challenger, sought the union's endorsement. In the months leading up to the 2018 midterm elections, the WTU polled its members on endorsement choices, organized candidate forums and livestreamed them on Facebook, and invited candidates to openly campaign at its events. Most of the union's endorsed candidates, including a retired teacher who ran for the SBOE, won the elections. The hope was that with union-friendly candidates on the council and on the SBOE, the union would stand a better chance of prevailing in its fiercest fight, which was being able to bargain on the evaluation instrument, IMPACT.

The 2018 election's aftermath was particularly beneficial to the WTU, especially at the level of the SBOE. Ruth Wattenberg, a retired employee of the AFT, was elected president of the Board; Markus Batchelor, ardent supporter of the union, was selected as vice president. With most of the Board working collaboratively with the union, Zachary Parker, the representative from Ward 5 whom the WTU had reluctantly endorsed due to his ties with Democrats for Education Reform, distinguished himself by not accepting invitations to address rank and file, causing members to feel snubbed. He also drew attention after being quoted in a *Washington Post* article in October 2019 in which he appeared to suggest that, in his conversations with teachers, they expressed support for IMPACT and believed it was a necessary evaluation tool. When these issues were brought to his attention, he clarified that he never expressed an opinion on IMPACT but was quoting three of four union members who spoke favorably of the evaluation instrument at an event that he convened in Ward 8. He also stated that he had heard the concerns over IMPACT from many other teachers that he had spoken with. He pledged to work in partnership with the WTU, and he pledged mutual support moving forward. However, he mended his relationship with the union by standing by its members during the COVID-19 pandemic as teachers fought DCPS over the reopening of schools to in-person learning. He would eventually earn the endorsement of the WTU in the 2022 midterm elections where he won a seat as the Ward 5 council member.

The 2020 elections cycle in the District of Columbia witnessed an unusually crowded field, especially for the at-large seat vacated by David Grosso, the chair of the education committee. While the incumbents ran largely unchallenged, the at-large seat and Ward 4 drew a lot of public attention. Candidates who sought the WTU's endorsement were required to complete and submit a questionnaire to the Committee on Political Education (COPE) and then attend a candidates' forum to promote their positions especially on education. On the morning on November 4, 2020, although 100% of the union's endorsed candidates did not prevail, there was general hope that a comfortable number of allies were both on the council and the SBOE. For any teacher who has followed education policy in the district, the departure of David Grosso and his alleged ties to the charters was well celebrated—to be celebrated with even more pomp and pageantry was the ascension of Janeese Lewis George, whom the WTU had fought hard to elect as a replacement for Grosso.

In Florida, where the state legislature and the governor embarked on book bans, censorship, and restricting or rewriting of curriculum, the Miami Dade Association of Teachers resorted to an education and organizing campaign to mitigate the threat. The strategy used by the local union was focused on school board races, on voting, and of course on protecting unions because of what they perceived as attacks on working people, unions rights, and contracts. The president of the United Teachers of Dade, Karla Hernadez-Mats, compared the threats faced by her education community to those posed by authoritarian movements in Haiti, the Dominican Republic, and Spain under Franco where school systems where defunded and books banned. She described her political approach as working to bring more people into the fold to understand the impact of their vote on policy. She and her allies wanted to make sure people understood that education is the cornerstone of a democracy, especially as some citizens generally do not consider education among the top three issues that would influence their vote for a candidate.

In 2018 for example she approached the local school board to find creative ways to create new revenues for education that were out of what the state offered. The proposed referendum on the subject went from the school board to the county commission and eventually on a ballot. Not only did the union organize to get the initiative passed, but it helped raise about half a million dollars for the campaign. Once the initiative passed, it generated a billion dollars to Miami Dade Public Schools, with the funds being specifically set aside for teacher pay and for security. The initiative was reapproved in 2022. Hernandez-Mats herself did run for public office as a way of gaining more influence for unions in the state of Florida, but even though she lost, she remains an influential voice in the political arena, especially when it comes to opposing unpopular policies.

At the national level, the AFT played an active role in the election of Joe Biden as President of the United States in 2020. AFT's leadership actively campaigned and encouraged its members to canvas for the Biden/Harris ticket which eventually won the election. The lead up to the 2024 election cycle was rather slow, but when Joe Biden dropped out of the race in July 2024, the energy level among union members shifted.

2024 Presidential Elections

The 2024 election cycle opened up with the Democratic party incumbent, Joseph Biden, whom the unions had helped elect in 2020, running unopposed in the primaries. He would eventually become the party's presumptive nominee and was preparing for the formal nomination by delegates at the convention in Chicago later in the summer. A poor debate performance on June 27 against his opponent Donald Trump sparked media criticism and a call within his own party to drop out of the race. The campaign thus suffered a deadly blow and lack of morale, with energy eventually leaving the candidate no choice but to step aside on July 21. This catapulted Vice President Kamala Harris to lead the party's ticket. The latter's accession to the top of the party's ticket reinvigorated the electorate and brought in a lot of energy from not only the base but members of the Republican party who opposed Donald Trump.

Throughout the calls by the media and members of Joseph Biden's party to step aside, the major unions stood with him, but as soon as he stepped aside, the AFT became the first major labor union to endorse his replacement.

Kamala Harris, United States Vice President (2020-2024) and Vice Presidential Candidate (2024)

This coincided with the union's 88th convention slated for Houston, Texas, and the Vice President did not hesitate to accept an invitation to speak to convention delegates. The union's 1.8 million members were instrumental in the 2020 election and did throw their support behind the 2024 ticket. The president of the union's inclusion in the speaker lineup for the Democratic National Convention was testament to just how valued the support of the union is and has traditionally been to Democratic tickets. The union's endorsement for candidates has traditionally come with a call to its members to support the endorsed candidate through all means including cash donations, canvassing, and voting. The union and its membership became even more energized when their former member, Minnesota Governor Tim Waltz, was selected as the running mate to Kamala Harris. Just like in 2020, the union president kicked off a national bus tour in support of the ticket with a suggested itinerary that took them through over 20 states. Although the outcome of the election was not what the union and its members anticipated, their support definitely made in difference in the final tally. Yes, the two candidates at the top of the ticket lost, but the messaging of the union on their issues—creating agency for parents and kids and support for organized labor and public education—won even in jurisdictions where President Biden lost.

COVID-19 Pandemic

The COVID-19 pandemic was a real test for policymakers for their allegiance to organized labor. As educators and their allies protested against DCPS's plans to reopen schools in the middle of the pandemic, some educators believed that Phil Mendelson, the Chairman of the City Council, and David Grosso, the chair of the Education Committee, stood on the sidelines and watched without intervening to support them. In addition to drive-by car caravan protests in front of the schools' chancellor's residence, Mayor Bowser's and Davis Grosso's residences were frequent stops. When the council finally decided to hold a hearing on schools' reopening on October 23, 2020, the chairman did not welcome any union witnesses but suggested that everyone submit written questions in advance. In protest, members of the union and their allies, including parents, held a protest rally on the steps of the city hall at the same time that the hearing was going on. Robert White, one of the union's strongest allies on the council and also a DCPS parent, addressed the rally before returning to the hearing. White showed unequivocal disdain for the chancellor's reopening plan and the lack of transparency associated with it; he vowed to fight on behalf of teachers and the community that he represented on the council. Eboni Rose Thompson, an SBOE candidate for Ward 7, and Mysiki Valentine, at-large SBOE candidate, also spoke at the rally in solidarity with their union ally.

Besides candidates who were running for office, a long-time union ally, at-large councilmember Elissa Silverman, who chaired the Committee on Labor and Workforce Development, became very instrumental in advocating on behalf of WTU members and affiliated school unions for a safe return to in-person learning during the pandemic. Before the new council could convene in January, she sought to introduce emergency legislation that would put in place mechanisms for DCPS to increase engagement, collaboration, and transparency with employees and other stakeholders.

Meeting several times with labor leaders to develop the legislation is what policymakers do. In this instance, although the chairman of the council would end up not bringing the legislation to the floor, it was politically gratifying for her. At election time, she obviously would remind labor leaders, and they would recall that she stood by them when they were in need. That's how you earn votes in politics. It is a game of give and take even if the giving on one end is simply an attempt at something that may or may not materialize. Smart politicians stick with their allies, show up at their events, and return for votes at election time.

Returned Favor

The 2020 election of Joe Biden and Kamala Harris, two union allies, was a payoff for the labor community, especially teachers' unions. The support for the ticket was even stronger due to Dr. Jill Biden's ties to the NEA as a long-time member. There is no doubt that as the campaigns were underway, qualified candidates in both the AFT and NEA positioned themselves for consideration as secretary of education should Joe Biden's ticket win. That certainly paid off. After the elections and during the transition of power, members of both unions were heavily involved in the process. Miguel Cardona, a former fourth grade teacher and administrator with ties to the NEA, was eventually appointed and confirmed as Secretary of Education. Understanding the needs of educators was one of the considerations for Cardona's appointment, and he surely made it a point of duty to surround himself with teachers and union loyalists.

One of his early priorities became reforming the Public Service Loan Forgiveness (PSLF) program to alleviate the burden of student loans not only for teachers and other educators, but also for other public servants. Although Cardona and the Biden administration take credit for the overhaul of PSLF program, this all stemmed from a lawsuit filed by the AFT against the previous administration for denying loan forgiveness to most of the applicants who qualified for the program. When the new administration came into office, it settled that lawsuit and created a one-year waiver that eventually paved the way for millions of public servants to take advantage of the benefit. Among the measures taken was the temporal pause on student loan repayments during the COVID-19 pandemic while still allowing those months of nonpayment to count toward forgiveness. This would lead to a historic number of borrowers' student loans being forgiven while getting others closer to the 120 payments required for forgiveness.

With a lot of anticipation and pressure from progressives for President Biden and his administration to cancel student loans, the administration took the extraordinary move to cancel $10,000 for borrowers earning under $125,000 and an additional $10,000 for those who benefitted from Pell grants. It is still unknown whether this move influenced the outcome of the 2022 midterm elections for Democrats, but the number of legal challenges to the cancellation was very noticeable. The U.S. Supreme court struck down this loan forgiveness program in 2023. There were separate lawsuits challenging the legality of some of the measures that President Biden and his administration took to reduce student loan debt. The challenges, however, did not stop the administration from continuing to encourage borrowers to apply for loan forgiveness. According to *educationdata.org*, a team of researchers that collect data and statistics about the U.S. education system, as of 2023, a total of 441,234 student loan borrowers had their loans forgiven through the Public Service Loan Forgiveness program (PSLF). Among that number, teacher loan forgiveness accounts for 22.1% for the total number forgiven through PSLF (Hanson, 2024). Separate reporting by media organizations reported approved cancellation of $169 billion in student loan debt for nearly 4.8 million borrowers through existing forgiveness programs. At the close of the Biden administration in December 2024, the President announced $4.28 billion in additional student loan relief for 55,000 borrowers, bringing the total in loan forgiveness numbers to an estimated $180 billion for nearly 5 million qualified borrowers enrolled in PSLF (Bilyeau, n.d.).

Whatever the outcome of the remaining legal challenges is, the Biden administration certainly made strides to maintain its teacher base that helped elect him to office and obviously did what is right for teachers. Although there might not have been sufficient success at meeting the needs of all educators and children around the country, it is evident that the Biden administration cared and continued to engage with this key voting block right up to the last days of his presidency with the signing of the Social Security Fairness Act.

In addition to student debt relief, the Biden administration through the Department of Education took several actions that will benefit teachers and the profession as a whole in the long term. Some of these actions over his four-year term included increasing funding for teacher preparation and teacher quality programs, directing resources to historically underserved schools through the Title I program, doubling federal funding to expand community schools—an initiative that unions are passionate about—and expanding access to mental health supports in schools, to name a few (U.S. Department of Education, n.d.). In State Houses, Illinois Governor J.B. Pritzker, Minnesota Governor and former vice presidential candidate, Tim Walz, and Wisconsin Governor, Tony Evers made significate increases to K–12 education funding in their 2023 budgets. In the city of Chicago, Mayor Brandon Johnson is on track to dramatically expand the number community schools in Chicago Public Schools through increased funding and community partnerships (Chicago Mayor's Office, 2025).

Further Reading

American Federation of Teachers. (n.d.). *We care. We fight. We show up. We vote. AND WE SAVE LIVES AND OUR DEMOCRACY.* https://www.aft.org/we-care-we-fight-we-show-we-vote-and-we-save-lives-and-our-democracy

Bilyeau, N.(n.d.). *"Student Loan Forgiveness: Programs for Relief and Forgiveness".* SoFi. https://www.sofi.com/student-loan-forgiveness-guide/

Chicago Mayor's Office. (2025). *Sustainable community schools.* Chicago.gov. https://www.chicago.gov/city/en/depts/mayor/press_room/press_releases/2025/july/sustainable-community-schools.html

Hanson, Melanie. "Student Loan Forgiveness Statistics" EducationData.org, August 28, 2024. https://educationdata.org/student-loan-forgiveness-statistics

Janus v. American Federation of State, County, and Municipal Employees, Council 31, 138 S. Ct. 2448 (2018).

Kim, Juliana (2023). "Florida says AP class teaches critical race theory. Here's what's really in the course." *NPR.*

Laveates, Matt (2024). "Transgender Bathroom Bills are Back: Does the nation care?" *NBC*

Levitz, Eric (2019). "Democracy Dies When Labor Unions Do" *New York Magazine.*

Social Security Fairness Act of 2023. H.R. 82. 118th Cong., 2nd sess., Enrolled Bill December 27, 2024.

Uetricht, Micah. "The Movement That Made Brandon Johnson Mayor of Chicago." The Nation, 2023.

U.S. Department of Education. (n.d.). *Teacher Quality Partnership Program.* https://www.ed.gov/grants-and-programs/teacher-preparation-grants/teacher-quality-partnership-program

CHAPTER 8

The Power of Protests and Resistance

Injustice anywhere is a threat to justice everywhere. We are caught in an inescapable network of mutuality, tied in a single garment of destiny. Whatever affects one directly, affects all indirectly.

— Martin Luther King, Jr.

Teachers and workers around the globe have generally considered their working conditions as oppressive, which has long been a rallying force for collective action. *The Pedagogy of the Oppressed* (Freire, et al., 2018) describes any situation where one party objectively exploits the other or "hinders his and her pursuit of self-affirmation as a responsible person" (p. 55) as oppression. The act of protesting or resisting oppression therefore constitutes fighting to be fully human. It is no doubt then that the quest for humanization, especially at the workplace, lays the foundation for labor. When that right to be fully human is threatened, the natural response is to protest, regardless of the form that the protest takes.

Paradoxically, the quest for social justice and better working conditions has resulted in the powerful posturing as victims. Diversity, Equity, and Inclusion initiatives have been deemed an attack on the majority racial group in the United States, even though the initiatives only seek to achieve a level playing field for all citizens. Critical Race Theory has been deemed offensive and mislabeled within right wing circles with false and unfounded claims. The election of Donald Trump as President of the United States of America in 2016 and his reelection in 2024 ushered in new threats to education equity and access. His campaign rhetoric was characterized by threats to public education and the dehumanizing and exclusion of students from various ethnic and national backgrounds. The inflammatory rhetoric targeting Mexican immigrants and Muslims in the lead-up to the 2016 election was particularly intimidating and created a lot of fear among students and families from these backgrounds.

Not only did the rhetoric and anticipated actions against students and educators from certain social groups create fear and anxiety, but it also energized teacher groups to mobilize to counter the planned assault. Amid the backdrop of imminent danger, the only option on the table became fighting back.

Betsy DeVos

Candidate Trump made good on his election promises by appointing an anti-public secretary of education to follow through with his agenda. Betsy Devos was no new name in the education arena. She had been an ardent advocate of school choice and private schools for 30 years, and there was no doubt in the minds of members of the labor community that she would not only siphon dollars from public schools to channel toward school choice but also pursue a policy agenda that did not favor the former.

As soon as DeVos was nominated, the two major teachers' unions, the AFT and the NEA, launched an opposition campaign in collaboration with their allies in Congress to stop her confirmation. Public education is the bedrock of our democracy, and having anyone in a role that would deprive any student of the right to a public education would have been devastating to me as a public-school teacher and a union building representative in 2017. I was initially contacted by AFT Communications and asked if I would be interested in delivering remarks not to exceed three minutes on the importance of public education and why Betsy DeVos would not be a good fit for my students and families. I unreluctantly accepted the role of speaker, but unbeknownst to me, they needed me to be the emcee for the event. When I arrived, there was a lot of media presence and a podium set up for speakers. I was handed a script with all the speakers who were U.S. senators, union leaders, parents, or K–12 students and asked to emcee the event.

Washington Teachers' Union Member, Terence Ngwa, hosting a political rally to oppose the confirmation of Betsy DeVos as Education Secretary (2017)

Speaker upon speaker voiced their opposition to the confirmation of President Trump's appointee and urged their senators to vote against the conformation. The sentiment from Randi Weingarten and Lily Eskelsen García, AFT and NEA presidents respectively, was similar—a firm rejection of Ms. DeVos's agenda over the past three decades and a call for their members to influence the vote through calls to their congressional representatives. Although Betsy DeVos went on to be confirmed as education secretary through a very tight vote that involved then Vice President Mike Pence voting to break the tie, she would go down as one of the most unpopular secretaries in recent times.

Educators around the country in the meantime did not give up on their opposition to her agenda. After almost a year in office, the AFT sent out a survey to its members to rate Ms. DeVos's performance which they in turn used to issue a report card. The items listed on the survey included full funding for the Department of Education and its programs, access and equity in public schools for all, the protection of students' civil rights, school improvement, and promoting gender equity on college campuses. The report card that was issued for Ms. DeVos and delivered by the AFT president and her allies was a symbolic move to oppose DeVos and the administration's policies and a way to disavow all that they represented.

Union Leaders and other activists attempt to deliver report cards to Betsy DeVos (2018)

Funding for DCPS Librarians

Advocacy for ensuring that there is a librarian at each DC public school dates back over a decade. Back in 2012, a petition to restore librarians to each school alleged that 57 schools serving about 16,500 students did not have a librarian. The schools' chancellor's proposed budget at the time accounted for only part-time librarians at 61% of the schools in the nation's capital. It is an issue that the union, whose members include librarians, continue to contend with. The issue took center stage again post-COVID-19 pandemic, prompting the union and its allies to again go on the offensive to protect students' rights to read through the availability of a full-time librarian at each school. Data collected by the WTU in 2021 estimated that at least 34 schools either didn't have a librarian or didn't have enough funding for a full-time position. As in the past, the union led the effort to initiate a petition to the city council to ensure that each school had a fully funded position for a school librarian, especially in the city's most disadvantaged Wards, 7 and 8. In addition to the petition and lobbying of allies at the city council, the librarians staged a silent read-in in front of the city hall, otherwise known as the Wilson Building. Not only did the union throw its weight behind this as a job-saving measure for its members, but it also pitched their advocacy around improving student literacy levels, especially among the school district's most vulnerable students who are Black and Latino.

Book Bans

The advent of book bans in right-wing jurisdictions around the country was a new low in what many believed amounted to an assault on individual rights and freedoms. Through misinformation and inflammatory language perpetrated by some Republicans in Congress, some members of the public were led to believe that young children in public schools were being exposed to content that was inappropriate. The incendiary accusations against public school libraries were that they were housing and teaching pornography in schools or steering young children toward same-sex relationships. In addition to storming school board meetings to have particular books taken off bookshelves, groups of parents also made requests to be involved in the selection of books and content that was taught in schools. This was further exacerbated by anti-DEI groups that disavowed content related to diversity, equity, and inclusion. Under pressure from parent groups, the Republican majority in the House of Representatives passed H.R. 5, Parents Bill of Rights, which gave parents, among other things, the right to a list of books and other reading materials contained in the library of their child's school and the right to inspect those books and other reading materials (Parents Bill of Rights Act, 2023). While parental involvement in education is beneficial, especially for school improvement purposes, and while parents have a right to decide which books their children can or cannot read, an inspection of books and other reading materials may result in a disruption to the smooth operation of libraries.

The state of Florida went even further by rejecting an Advanced Placement course covering African American history. The Florida Department of Education argued that the course wasn't about the teaching of history but about an agenda to indoctrinate students to a political agenda. The immediate uproar was evident with the major teachers' unions stepping up opposition to the limitations to what content students were given access to. In March 2024, the United Teachers of Dade under the leadership of Karla Hernandez-Mats participated in the Comparative International Education Society's (CIES's) annual convening in Miami Florida, themed *The Power of Protest*, to oppose the state's book bans. Conference attendees joined Ms. Hernandez-Mats and her national president in protest by taking to the streets, each with a copy of a book with content that could possibly make it ineligible to be taught at any of Florida's schools. This public show of defiance against the state government put the teachers' union at the forefront of advocacy for a social justice cause. Panel discussions on the Politics of Hate and sessions that opposed the state's book ban helped to raise awareness of the need to organize against racism and provide a platform for educators, parents, and youth to work toward educational and social justice. Ms. Hernandez-Mats's decision to involve CIES conference attendees in the protest was a way of catapulting a local issue to the global stage where more people could be sensitized and educated on the issue, and consequently be part of the many voices advocating for rolling back the limitations on access to books (Hernandez-Mats, personal communication, 2025).

Allies against book bans in the state of Florida include Pan America, Families Against Book Bans, Moms for Libros, among others. In July 2024, Pan America organized a summit in Orlando called United Voices Summit. The over 350 attendees—teachers, librarians, parents, students, and community members—convened to be educated on the impact of book bans on educators and students and obtained resources to help them fight back, especially at the ballot box (Hernandez-Mats, personal communication, 2025). *Moms for Libros* is a counter for *Moms for Liberty* and their agenda. These are parents who connect with unions and other social justice groups to jointly organize to fight back against policies that affect their communities. Because people generally don't put education at the top of their local and national election-related issues, unions participate in events like this to educate the electorate on how to use their vote as a protest against legislation they oppose. Teachers' unions consider education a cornerstone of democracy, and getting education right helps democracy to thrive.

AFT and First Book Partnership

Unions by and large, even though not required, provide support to their members in schools with the goal of improving teaching and learning. In addition to professional development and various grants, unions have stepped up their support for students by providing much needed supplies at critical moments. One of the most notable supports has been the partnership between the AFT and the non-profit group, *First Book*, that has provided millions of books to students around the country. In the era of book bans, although there has been no specific mention of this effort as a protest measure to counter the actions of legislatures vis-à-vis these bans, the AFT has drastically increased its supply of books to schools through *First Book* (First Book Staff, 2024).

Different local union leaders have touted the profound impact that these books have had on students in their districts. Supporting literacy for students is paramount to the work that unions do, and far beyond using books to protest book bans, they make age-appropriate books available to students without any restrictions. During the COVID-19 pandemic, these books were particularly useful to students as schools shut down and they studied virtually from home. Teachers braved the fear of contamination and set up open air distribution points for their students to pick up books to read while at home.

Attacks on LGBTQ Youth

On July 1, 2022, another unpopular law called the "Don't Say Gay" law went into effect in the same state of Florida. The law's stated purpose was "to prohibit classroom discussion about sexual orientation or gender identity in certain grade levels or in a specified manner" (Florida Legislature, 2022, p. 1). This new policy is also embedded throughout the Florida Education Code by defining "sex" as "the classification of a person as either female or male based on the organization of the body of such person for a specific reproductive role, as indicated by the person's sex chromosomes, naturally occurring sex hormones, and internal and external genitalia present at birth" (Florida Legislature, 2024, p. 1). In response to these attacks on LGBTQ students and their educators, the two major teachers' unions issued guidance to their members and publicly challenged these perceived violations of federal civil rights protections for students and staff. Restrictions on LGBTQ youth have been in place in Republican jurisdictions since 2016 when the nation was shocked and decried outright discrimination after North Carolina passed a transgender bathroom ban. Nine other states passed similar transgender bathroom ban bills, the most recent being Utah in 2024. Again, the two major teachers' unions have been at the forefront, pushing their allies to protest and seek a repeal of these bills to protect civil liberties for all.

So far, teachers' unions have taken an active role in protesting, resisting, and legally challenging legislation geared toward limiting the rights of students and educators. Several legal victories in the state of Florida against the state's "antiwoke" legislation have set the path for resistance in other jurisdictions. The Florida Circuit Court for example ruled against the constitutionality of the legislation, forcing the state's governor to roll it back. Equality Florida, a key ally of the UTD, has been very vocal against this anti LGBTQ+ legislation and considered the circuit court's decision a major win for the community. The Florida Education Association has a pending lawsuit against Senate Bill 256 which impacts public employees and discriminates against certain employees having a right to union representation. In addition to these collective challenges, individual teachers have stood up against the state's government. This was the case of a Jacksonville teacher who refused to take down her Black Lives Matter (BLM) sign from the classroom and was terminated as a consequence. After taking legal action, the courts ruled in her favor, reinstated her with back pay, and cleared her of any wrongdoing.

Teachers' unions have historically used the organizing model to rally allies to coalesce around them to stand up against actions they deem unfavorable to their members. What is different now is that the resistance is broader and is messaged around the protection of democracy and individual and group freedoms. Traditionally, protests and resistance have culminated in strike action or work stoppage, but antistrike clauses in state constitutions and collective bargaining agreements that come with stiff penalties for violations have forced teachers' unions to be more creative.

Florida's state constitution is one of those that prohibit any type of strike or collective action that can lead to work stoppage. One of those creative methods of resistance has been forging alliances with people and organizations they typically wouldn't align with. For example, parent groups, Equality Florida, Prizm, the National Association for the Advancement of Colored People (NAACP), and the Florida Interfaith Alliance have been among some of the most vocal groups working with the teachers' unions and other unions to protest government actions.

School Closures

School choice has resulted in an uptick in the closure of traditional public schools in predominantly Black jurisdictions in the country. In the District of Columbia, those areas are located in the northeast and southeast parts of the city. The closures usually follow a pattern of low attendance, declining enrollment, low student achievement, and lack of resources, which eventually lead to the creation of smaller charter schools to accommodate the students, or the students are absorbed by other schools neighboring them. The vacant spaces created by the school closures end up occupied through leases by charter schools.

The district's chancellors, past and present, and some members of the city council have characterized the closures as cost-saving measures. Since 1990, about 72 public schools have closed with at least 43 occurring after 2007 (Jablow, 2023). The majority of the space is currently occupied by charter schools. For many years, the Washington Teachers' Union and its allies have decried and protested this pattern to maintain the makeup of traditional public schools in the city. In early 2020 when it became evident that Washington Metropolitan Alternative High School would be closed, the union was at the forefront of the protests to keep it open, circulating a petition that garnered 1,600 signatures and the president of the union issuing a statement condemning the closure (Washington Teachers' Union, 2019). She characterized the closure as a failure of school and city officials to invest in the school, further destabilizing already-vulnerable students. In an unusual move, she provided transportation to students who were willing to take an unexcused absence to deliver the signed petition to the city's mayor and the City Council. Although the State of Board of Education was sympathetic to the union's and students' cause, the body unfortunately was powerless and couldn't reverse the closure given that the schools are overseen by the city administration rather than the board.

Protests of this nature follow a similar pattern in the south side of Chicago where parent groups such as the Journey for Justice, a major union ally, have joined forces for many years to protest school closures. While the protests have failed to dissuade public officials from keeping most of the schools closed, the unions have at least brought public attention to the inadequate funding of public education.

COVID-19 Protections

When D.C. public schools and schools around the country closed their doors in March 2020 and resorted to virtual learning due to the COVID-19 pandemic, there was a lot of uncertainty and anxiety among educators and parents. While the latter were angry because of the ensuing learning loss, teachers and other educators were anxious about returning to their school buildings, especially when it became evident that the virus disproportionately affected older people. With the public pressure for students to return to in-person learning came resistance from teachers' unions, something that up to today remains a cloud on the union leadership: union busters blaming them for depriving students of learning. The process of negotiating a return for teachers to serve their students in the city's traditional public schools exposed a lot of facilities issues, especially around air quality, an issue that had hitherto not been in the spotlight. As union leaders and their allies joined school leaders to inspect schools for measures taken to improve air quality, some union rank-and-file members embarked on protests to keep the schools closed, their doubts emanating from the general lack of trust for school officials.

American Federation of Teachers and Washington Teachers' Union presidents tour McKinley Technology High School during the COVID-19 Pandemic to review health protections.

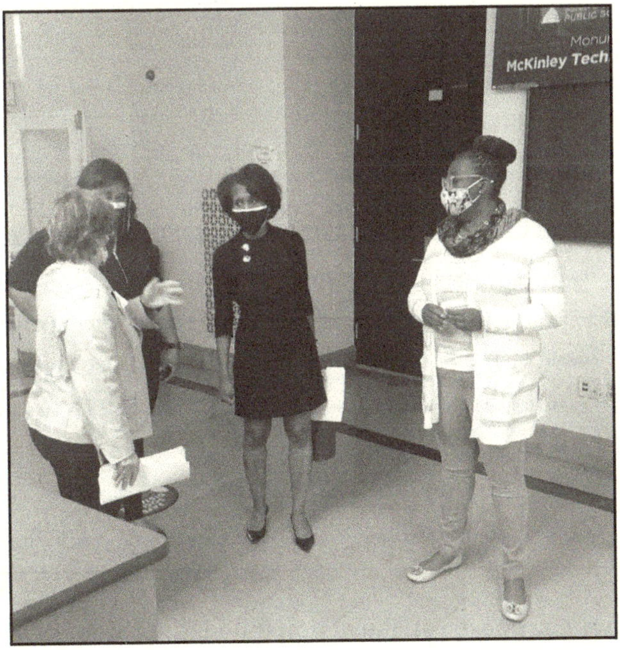

While the union leadership mounted pressure on the district through negotiations and organized protests in public spaces, some of their members resorted to picketing in front of the homes of the schools'

chancellor and other influential city officials. One year of negotiating terms of reopening the schools did not convince union members that the buildings were safe. When union members defied leadership by voting down a proposed reopening Memorandum of Agreement with the school district and threatened to force the union to go on strike, the district filed a restraining order against the move (DC v. WTU – TRO Motion, 2021).

Copy of The District of Columbia's Emergency Motion for Temporary Restraining Order against the Washington Teachers' Union (2021).

SUPERIOR COURT OF THE DISTRICT OF COLUMBIA
CIVIL DIVISION

DISTRICT OF COLUMBIA, ***Plaintiff,*** v. **WASHINGTON TEACHERS' UNION, LOCAL #6 AMERICAN FEDERATION OF TEACHERS, AFL-CIO,** ***Defendant.***	**Case No.** ________ **Judge** _____ **Calendar** ___ **Next Event:** ______________

THE DISTRICT OF COLUMBIA'S
EMERGENCY MOTION FOR TEMPORARY RESTRAINING ORDER

The District of Columbia (District) moves under Super Ct. Civ. R. 12-I(b)(6) and D.C. Code § 1-617.05 for a temporary restraining order preventing the Washington Teachers' Union Local #6, American Federation of Teachers, AFL-CIO and District teachers from engaging in a strike or work stoppage that would halt the District's reopening of some schools for in-person learning on February 2, 2021.

The grounds and the reasons for the District's requested relief are set forth in the accompanying memorandum of points and authorities. A prop[illegible]porary Restraining Order

Although the proposed strike action failed, the threat in and of itself, coupled with organized protests supported by allies, put the union and its members in a better negotiating position.

The labor movement has historically used the power of protest to effect much-needed change not only at the workplace but also within the larger scope of enhancing the democratic process. Protests, whether successful or not in achieving union demands, fall within a broader strategy of bringing public attention to workplace issues and garnering their support. For teachers' unions, the framing matters, especially shining the light on gaps that affect student learning and seeking the sympathy and support of parents.

Further Reading

DC v. WTU - TRO Motion - 2-1-2021. (2021). *Emergency motion for temporary restraining order.* D.C. Sup. Ct.

District of Columbia Geographic Information System. (n.d.). Closed Public Schools. DC Open Data. https://opendata.dc.gov/datasets/DCGIS::closed-public-schools/

First Book Staff. (2024). *AFT gives away 10 million books to help create a generation of joyful, confident readers.* First Book. https://firstbook.org/blog/2024/05/11/aft-gives-away-10-million-books-to-help-create-a-generation-of-joyful-confident-readers

Florida Legislature. (2022). *CS/CS/HB 1557: Parental Rights in Education* [Bill text]. https://www.flsenate.gov/Session/Bill/2022/1557/BillText/er/PDF

Florida Legislature. (2024). *Florida Statutes § 456.001: Definitions.* https://www.leg.state.fl.us/Statutes/index.cfm?App_mode=Display_Statute&URL=0400-0499/0456/Sections/0456.001.html

Florida Statutes. (n.d.). § 1001.21(9)

Florida Statutes. (2020). § 1000.071(1)

Florida Senate. (2023). SB 256: Florida Senate 2023 Regular Session. https://www.flsenate.gov/Session/Bill/2023/256

Freire, P., Ramos, M. B., Macedo, D. P., & Shor, I. (2018). *Pedagogy of the oppressed.* 50th anniversary edition. New York, Bloomsbury Academic.

H.R.5 - 118th Congress (2023-2024): Parents Bill of Rights Act. (2023, March 27). https://www.congress.gov/bill/118th-congress/house-bill/5

Jablow, V. (2023). *Planning for schools and saving them, Part 1: DCPS closures* [Blog post]. EducationDC. https://educationdc.net/2023/02/09/planning-for-schools-and-saving-them-part-1-dcps-closures

King, M. L., Jr. (1963). *Letter from Birmingham Jail.* https://www.africa.upenn.edu/Articles_Gen/Letter_Birmingham.html

Washington Teachers' Union. (2019). *Statement on closure of Washington Metropolitan Opportunity Academy.* https://www.wtulocal6.net/statement_on_closure_of_washington_met

CHAPTER 9

Challenging Times

You must be the change you wish to see in the world.

— Mahatma Gandhi

Those who are familiar with the inner workings of unions certainly understand that they operate like traditional family structures. From minor disagreements to power grabs or ambitions, it is not unusual for rank and file, some of whom become disgruntled or overly ambitious, to stage opposition to leadership. That obviously results in infighting, backstabbing, and disunity within some circles. While union busters have played a key role in demonizing, destabilizing, and attempting to weaken organized labor, union members themselves have been their own worst enemies, which is not unusual given that they operate as a family structure.

Because disagreements within teachers' unions are not uncommon, I will not attempt to identify individual unions where this is commonplace. Rather, I will focus on what has taken place within the Washington Teachers' Union over the years that has been newsworthy. This has ranged from financial malfeasance to power struggles.

Financial Malfeasance

In December 2002, the WTU was involved in a financial scandal that attracted the attention of the FBI, IRS, U.S. Department of Labor, and the D.C. Inspector General, all of which became involved in an extensive investigation. This scandal rocked the union world and would go down as one of the most egregious happenings in the history of organized labor that relies on member dues for subsistence. Then WTU president Barbara A. Bullock of blessed memory, her treasurer, James O. Baxter III, her personal assistant, Gwendolyn M. Hemphill, and her chauffeur, Leroy Holmes, were accused of swindling an estimated $5 million dollars from the union's treasury. According to court records, the American Federation of Teachers (AFT), the parent organization of the WTU, brought suit against Bullock and her co-defendants for engaging in a financial scheme that resulted in the embezzlement of funds from the local. Bullock, who served as president from mid-1994 to September 2002, was empowered with financial responsibility over the union's day-to-day operations, including check-signing authority which she shared with the treasurer.

One of the standard practices within AFT locals is to remit monthly per capita payments to the parent organization. The per capita payment is calculated based on the membership of the local, and the AFT has worked tirelessly over the years to keep membership numbers at acceptable levels to ensure that the locals do not default on payment. In the case of Bullock and her associates embezzling money from the WTU treasury, the AFT was severely harmed because part of its revenue stream emanates from the per capita dues paid by affiliates.

After the indictment and imprisonment of the defendants, the WTU went into receivership. During the receivership period, the AFT oversaw the operations of the WTU until the time when the latter could demonstrate that it could manage its own affairs with integrity.

The post-scandal and receivership leadership featured George Parker and Nathan Saunders as president and vice president respectively in 2005. That administration coincided with the election of Adrian Fenty as Mayor of Washington D.C. and the eventual transition to mayoral control of the schools. Despite the controversies surrounding Chancellor Michelle Rhee, Mr. Parker endorsed her brash style and endorsed her transformative vision of reducing the power of teacher seniority and the introduction of the new teacher evaluation system, IMPACT. Parker's behavior put him at odds with his own membership and the leadership of the AFT. He eventually went on to work with Michelle Rhee after an electoral defeat by his own vice president, Nathan Saunders. His professional alliance with

Michelle Rhee and his support for charter schools has demonstrated the hypocrisy of one who was once the voice of the labor movement in a city known for its place in the history of the labor movement in the District of Columbia (Sawchuk, 2011).

Power Struggle

The bad blood within the union's leadership did not end with Parker and Saunders. Saunders would end up as a one-term president after a defeat by Elizabeth Davis in 2013. Even with internal division spearheaded by her own vice president, Candi Peterson, and constant opposition by her predecessor, Davis led the union through the most stable period in its history. Although she was admired by many within the rank and file, managed the resources of the union judiciously, and gained national recognition within her union leadership peer group, that did not deter her vice president from opposing her. Peterson would eventually stage electoral challenges against Davis, losing both times. Infighting within the executive board and backstabbing led to mistrust and delays in decision-making for the three terms that Davis led the local. Because of the history of backstabbing, she kept the two vice presidents who served her furthest from decision-making and used them more as field services specialists. The vice presidents under Davis were more like figureheads than close collaborators due to the almost obsessive fear of sabotage. Davis's mistrust for her vice presidents and other members of her executive board were a constant source of anxiety and sensitivity for her. She was particularly sensitive to members of her own team staging a challenge against her in each of the elections and intentionally kept those whose views aligned with hers close and those who could become potential challengers at bay, leading to a lot of consternation.

It was during Davis's leadership that some disgruntled members of the executive board, without consultation with their colleagues, formed the DC Caucus of Rank-and-File Educators (DC CORE). Inspired by the ideals of Labor Notes, a Chicago-based organization that sought to empower union members to be more active, and the Caucus of Rank-and-File Educators, a subgroup of the Chicago

Teachers' Union, the D.C. group became a force to reckon with during the COVID-19 pandemic. Initially, the group was perceived as an opposition group whose mission was to topple the current administration, but as their activities unfolded, it became clear that they simply wanted to be at the table and to instill more democratic values within the union.

According to the leadership of the group, they were more interested in empowering rank and file members to be more involved in their union. The lack of racial diversity within the group and its insensitivity to issues affecting teachers of color inspired another group of teachers to form the Black Caucus of Rank-and-File Educators (B-CORE). Initially, the leadership of the WTU sought the help of the AFT to quash the activities of the group as illegal, but the latter distanced itself from the internal issues of the local. After all, the founders of DC CORE argued that AFT benefitted electorally from the Progressive Caucus, of which WTU's president was a member. The fear of DC CORE staging a challenge in elections was sort of credible, given that the same structure (coached and mentored by Labor Notes) within the ranks of the Baltimore Teachers' Union had resulted in the defeat of its longtime president Marietta English. With the energy garnered through the movement, members of DC CORE through their organizing were initially elected to key positions on the executive board leading up to the 2025 elections when Laura Fuchs, a longtime recording secretary and key voice of the group, ousted the incumbent president by 56% to 37% of the reported votes (Washington Teachers' Union, 2025).

Organizational Leadership and Management Training

Many union leaders start up as prominent activists within rank-and-file members. Activists and agitators have their place in the labor movement, but beyond the high energy and ability to rile up a crowd lies the Herculean task of navigating organizational bureaucracies. Serving as a building representative for the union or being on a committee or contract negotiating team does not prepare one for leading a 5,000-member organization with all its diverse needs. Like those in many organizations, union leaders have to juggle multiple responsibilities which entail the political, the relational, and the organizational.

One of the gaps I witnessed within the leadership of the WTU, which I believe is not unique to this local, is lack of preparation for the role of president and vice president. The minimum requirement to run for office is being a member in good standing and collecting signatures from colleagues to validate one's candidacy. Some leaders grew in the role by taking advantage of professional development opportunities at higher institutions of learning and those offered by their parent organizations. The visible lack of understanding of basic organizational theory continues to plague the local union to date, especially in the areas of staffing, supervision, and financial management. Unions have continuously pressed for employers to invest in mentoring programs, and I believe, they would better serve their members by intentionally investing in training and mentoring opportunities for their leaders. Although the AFT provides opportunities through the Scheinman Institute at Cornell University, they are limited; nevertheless, individual leaders or their local unions can benefit from a minimum investment in a course lineup that would empower them with the effective execution of their duties. Running an understaffed headquarters, the inability to properly supervise and hold staff accountable, the lack of financial acuity, and the overreliance on lawyers, at a high financial cost, negatively impact the services rendered to members as well as union culture in general.

Challenging Employees and Lawsuits

One of the challenges that plagued the WTU, at least during my time, was the unending lawsuits originating from current and former employees and current and former members over representation issues. For a labor organization, there is an expectation that as an employer, it would live up to the ideals of its mission and treat employees with the same degree of fairness it expects from its members' employer. Unfortunately, due to supervisor oversight or overreach, the union was entangled in a wage theft complaint—an offense that is not treated lightly in the District of Columbia—which fortunately was quickly corrected and settled, and all affected employees were compensated for the extra hours that they had worked without pay.

As in many organizations, employees who lacked commitment to their jobs made the role of supervisors more difficult than it needed to be. Issues with tardiness, gossips, unauthorized sharing of protected information, timeliness in the delivery of services to members, and other forms of unprofessional behavior created a work culture that sometimes became very challenging. Before joining the union office as executive director, I did a practicum for my doctoral program the year before that culminated in an employee accountability plan that I submitted to the president for consideration. The problems that plagued the office prior to my arrival persisted but with the exception that I put more accountability checks in place, though not as effectively as I would have loved to, due to interference by elected officers. Disciplinary measures taken against ineffective employees went from being managerial issues to becoming executive board agenda items by overzealous board members. While some employees resigned on their own for failure to perform at the expected levels, at least one returned with a frivolous lawsuit that dragged on for a long time and was carried by some print media organizations. Thanks to proper documentation, computer forensics, and legal representation, the union survived a lawsuit that would have greatly scarred its image, especially given that the grounds for this suit were based on discrimination against a protected class. The former employee in this case, who had been terminated during his probationary period, brought suit against the union president Elizabeth Davis and Dorothy Egbufor, the Chief of Staff (COS), in 2018, alleging that he was subjected to a hostile work environment and terminated because of his sexual identity. Because of fissures within the executive board and animosity against the COS by some of its members who wrote letters of recommendation for the plaintiff for his next job, he felt emboldened to proceed with the suit. Although the union ended up prevailing, it came at a huge financial cost in legal fees. Motivated by some of these lawsuits, some former and current members who had ongoing grievances or had lost their grievances against their employer, D.C. Public Schools, either threatened to sue or sued the union for perceived lack of representation.

Support for Leaders with Substance Abuse Challenges

The history of substance abuse, be it be it legal or illegal substances, by people in power is nothing new and spans over several decades. As popular and admired as Marion Barry was as mayor of the District of Columbia, that popularity was overshadowed by his personal shortcomings, especially around the use of drugs. It is an epidemic that has plagued the United States for so long, ranging from crack cocaine in the 1980s to the modern-day opioid crisis. While there have been disparities in the approach to these crises around racial lines, the fact remains that all individuals regardless of race or creed are vulnerable to substance abuse and should be given equal attention.

Elizabeth Ann Davis, fondly known as "Liz," was a very knowledgeable, articulate, hardworking, and well-respected member of the local and national labor community. Her popularity and knowledge of education and education policy featured her on many panels hosted by members of the education community. She was fun-loving and cared about the people around her but also held them to very high standards as she did with herself. As hardworking as she was, she was also human and susceptible to shortcomings just like any of us. In addition to the job-embedded protections that she advocated for on behalf of her members, she was a champion of wellness, partnering with Recovery Centers for America to support members with substance abuse problems and encouraging members to use employer-provided mental health services through INOVA during the COVID-19 pandemic. As a social drinker just like many of us, there was really nothing unusual to take home besides what everyone did to relax after their long day. Throughout my tenure as her close collaborator, I could not in my wildest imagination have thought that one day, part of her legacy would be marred by stories of alcohol abuse.

A few weeks leading up to Liz's reelection to a third term, information surfaced from local newspapers regarding her alleged role in a late-night car crash involving the use of alcohol, otherwise known as Driving Under the Influence (DUI). This empowered one of her long-time rivals, Nathan Saunders, with ammunition to go after her.

It is possible that Davis's alcohol use was known among a close circle of individuals, but because of the sensitivity of the issue and her strong personality, probably no one really bothered to confront her about it, or she might have pushed back when the subject came up.

As a close collaborator in my role as executive director, I was in the conference room with her when a staff member broke the news of Saunders going public about the issue of her DUI, which I obviously wasn't aware of at the time. Although she did take the phone off speaker, there was no way to conceal it from me, and she immediately sprung into damage control mode. Not only was it devastating to her, but it was also embarrassing to those closest to her professionally.

For a long time, Saunders had alleged in his campaigns that the president had missed critical meetings with key stakeholders due to her alcohol use, but no one believed him at the time and regarded those pronouncements as mere campaign rhetoric intended to blackmail his opponent. This situation was a very unfortunate occurrence in the life of the popular union president, but nothing that should be construed as reckless behavior. She embodied the earmarks of a profession that worsens substance abuse—the long work hours, the stress from demanding members, the lack of trusted individuals, and other unknown factors. Many lives and careers would be saved if each union invested in mental health and substance abuse supports for their leaders and members.

Alcoholism and drug addiction are issues that plague many individuals and require empathy and care in the way they are approached. When carefully handled, individuals can elect to seek the necessary treatment without fear of being stigmatized or embarrassed. Davis's situation was not the latter, as her opponent used the situation to embarrass her, staging demonstrations with his supporters in front of the union's headquarters and the AFT headquarters even though no one at the parent organization was involved in the situation. The scandal and demonstrations notwithstanding, Davis would go on to win another term, defeating Saunders.

Catastrophe Strikes

On the morning of April 5, 2021, I woke up to several missed phone calls on both my work and personal cell phones. One of them was from the union's Communications Director, Joey Weedon, and the other from a *Washington Post* local reporter, Perry Stein. Perry was a very skillful and aggressive reporter whom I avoided at all costs because I was restricted from speaking to the media without authorization from the president and because of her questioning style and reporting. The voicemail message she left sought to match a car that was involved in a crash the previous night with its perceived owner, Liz Davis, before she could run a story on the accident. The description she provided as well as the location of the accident by all accounts matched Liz's car, and there was no doubt in my mind the identity of one of the victims in the crash was hers. When I called the Communications Director, he did not mince words in breaking the news as he had received it—Liz was involved in an accident late on Easter Sunday and did not make it.

My mind wondered for a moment, and my thoughts went back in time to her previous involvement with alcohol that had resulted in a minor accident. She and I had exchanged text messages on Easter Sunday, but there was no way I could have imagined those messages would be the last. Chills ran down my spine, and for a moment, I felt helpless, but when I recollected my emotions, I realized, Liz wouldn't have wanted the union to undergo any moment of instability, and I felt the obligation to ensure I was executing the full responsibilities of my role. After making several phone calls, I hopped behind the wheel to meet with the General Vice President, the General Counsel, the Communications Director, and a representative of the AFT.

The tragic loss of the Union President took many by surprise and opened the doors for some to create a caricature of her and demonize her without understanding the true picture of union culture.

In an environment where term limits are not the norm, ascending to leadership for some sometimes requires extreme measures to seek the office. The fear of losing a grip on power has created and continues to create paranoia among some union leaders as they constantly shield themselves from challengers within their ranks. Under this type of environment, trust is a very scarce virtue, and backstabbing, the norm. Being extremely sensitive and paranoid about being challenged was not an Elizabeth Davis invention—she worried about members of her executive board staging a challenge against her, especially with one of those members being visibly and actively involved in DC CORE. After all, her former challenger, Nathan Saunders, had previously used her DUI to blackmail her. How then could she have sought professional help for alcohol shortcomings, if any, knowing that her opponents would weaponize this against her or that members of the local media would make a story out of it that could potentially hurt her chances of continuing to lead the union?

Many powerful leaders have had shortcomings in different areas from drug use, to alcoholism, to inappropriate relationships, yet society has continued to castigate them rather than provide support. Members of teachers' unions and other labor groups can use their brotherhood/sisterhood slogan of "solidarity forever" to support one another and their leaders who may struggle with conditions that are commonplace in society and use their shared humanity to support them rather embark on smear campaigns that culminate in embarrassment, feelings of low self-esteem, insecurity, and tragedy. The handholding at rallies and picket lines should be a demonstration of brotherliness and support for one another in good and bad times. Moving beyond personal attacks, retaliation, and backstabbing would refocus energy on the things that matter most for the movement. Fulfilling the overall mission of the union, in the case of teachers' unions, advocating for better working conditions for their members, supporting and defending the rights of historically marginalized student populations, seeking equitable learning conditions for all students, being at the frontlines of social justice initiatives such as putting an end to gun violence, and continuously holding policymakers to task for providing equitable funding for all schools would lead to more respect and support for the movement.

Challenging times, whether personal or professional, call for changes in how business is conducted moving forward. I believe the leadership and personal challenges involving union leaders that I've recounted in this chapter will not constitute a referendum on all union leaders, but will help current and aspiring leaders to refocus on the mission of supporting and upholding the ideals of a free and equitable public education, championing social justice initiatives, and being at the service of both their members and the communities that they serve.

Further Reading

Baca, N. (2019, May 29). Washington Teachers Union President cited for DUI. ABC7

Gallagher, J. (2021, May 28). Washington Teachers' Union president at fault in fatal crash, police say. *WTOPNews*.

Sawchuk, S. (2011). *Rhee teams up with former union chief Parker. Education Week*. https://www.edweek.org/teaching-learning/rhee-teams-up-with-former-union-chief-parker/2011/05

Stein, P. (2019, June 18). Elizabeth Davis reelected as Washington Teachers' Union leader. *The Washington Post*.

Stein, P. & Hedgpeth, D. (2021, May 28). Washington Teachers' Union president was speeding and driving intoxicated at time of fatal crash, police say. *The Washington Post*.

Stein, P. (2019, May 29). Contentious Teachers Union Race draws attention to incumbent's DUI. *The Washington Post*.

Washington Teachers' Union. (2025). *WTU elections*. https://www.wtulocal6.net/wtu_elections

CHAPTER 10

The Road Ahead

In September 2019, Eric Levitz published an article in *New York* magazine titled *Unions Have Won the War of Ideas. Will That Win Them Power?* (Levitz, 2019). The article prompted me to dive into reflection mode as to what was still left to be done, not only to strengthen teachers' power, but to grow their numbers to a level that becomes a firewall. At a time when anti-union sentiment continues to be commonplace, particularly among right-wing politicians and their supporters, there is still a lot of work to be done. When the Supreme Court gutted workers' groups' ability to collect dues, there was limited hope for the survival of the movement. More than five years after the decision, paradoxically, Republican candidates for the White House courted some unions for their endorsement and did so successfully. Such outreach was a sign that numbers matter, and the reason for soliciting those endorsements was not only due to the power that those unions wield, but the number of members that they can turn out to the polls and convert to actual votes. Additionally, the 2024 elections proved that although unions have traditionally voted democratic, some of their members voted for the opposite party while holding on to their union ideals and values. As AFT president Randi Weingarten put it, "When labor and public education were on the ballot, they won regardless of whether Donald Trump won" (Weingarten, 2025, personal communication). She added while reacting to the outcome of the elections that "people want public services; people want a strong labor movement. People want public education. We want to fight for the values that we stand for and fight back when someone tries to take away our rights" (Weingarten, 2025, personal communication).

The recent state of affairs in Washington, D.C. demonstrates that a lot of work needs to be done. The Republican candidate for president and current President of the United States Donald Trump ran on a platform that threatened to disband the Department of Education and expand school choice. In the first few days of the administration, funds were frozen to some basic services which if not paused by a judge would have deprived many public school students of basic services. Title I schools and student disability services that are funded through the Individuals with Disabilities Education Act (IDEA), the HeadStart Program, the Supplemental Nutrition Assistance Program, and Community Schools would have been the most effected. Even in deeply conservative jurisdictions that voted overwhelmingly for the President, the thought of students missing out on basic services sent chills down everyone's spine. As the President followed through with the partial dismantling of the Department of Education backed by the U.S. Supreme Court, the unions continued to oppose his agenda more vigorously than they did during his first term with Betsy DeVos as Education Secretary. As defenders of traditional public schools, unions' opposition to school choice, which has already taken center stage with groups of advocates attending White House meetings, will be relentless. The amount of money siphoned from public schools to fund charter schools and vouchers is beyond measure, yet proponents perceive it as a way of curing the nation's K–12 education crisis. As unions and other advocates of traditional public schools have argued, allocating equitable resources and investing more in these schools would make a difference.

As diversity, equity, and inclusion (DEI) initiatives are attacked and dismantled at the federal and local levels, students from historically marginalized backgrounds will see opportunities disappear in favor of initiatives that disproportionately favor the racial majority in the United States. There is no question in my mind that the major teachers' unions and their locals will amplify their messaging around equity, rightfully so, in the next four years of the Trump administration as it pushes through its school choice agenda, dismisses lawsuits brought against school districts and state governments for banning books, and purges institutions of DEI initiatives.

Immigration is another unifying and organizing factor for teachers' unions whose members, their students, and parents have been the victims of Customs and Immigration Enforcement (ICE) agents under all White House administrations. The only difference is that under Donald Trump, immigration has become a demonizing and rallying force for his supporters, and he has used it to create immense trepidation in immigrant communities. Worse still, teachers and other educators will now have to contend with ICE raids in their schools which hitherto were among protected spaces that include places of worship and hospitals. Already, the education community is feeling the brunt of the raids, as a teacher in Miami Dade added to the growing list of parent victims in communities around the country. After being detained by ICE, the teacher was deported to Honduras in February 2025. In Chicago, ICE agents were turned away from Hamline Elementary School on day 4 of the new administration.

Chicago Teachers Union Tweet regarding attempted ICE entry at Hamline Elementary School (2025).

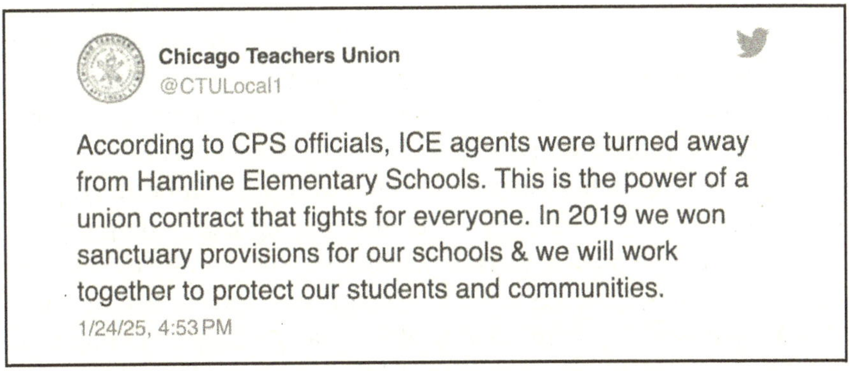

Chicago Teachers Union
@CTULocal1

According to CPS officials, ICE agents were turned away from Hamline Elementary Schools. This is the power of a union contract that fights for everyone. In 2019 we won sanctuary provisions for our schools & we will work together to protect our students and communities.

1/24/25, 4:53 PM

In preparation for President Trump's inauguration for a second term on January 20, 2025, teachers' unions built on their response to policies from his first term to prepare resources for schools and families. *The Know Your Rights* card (American Federation of Teachers, 2025) was a readily available resource for families to use when confronted with an ICE raid. As with other initiatives that labor and management have previously collaborated on, it is likely that they will do the same to protect their students and communities, especially in sanctuary cities like Chicago and New York City.

At a more personal level, when I left the K–12 space in 2021, I did not leave my union voice at the door. As a higher education professional at a school of education, preparing educators will be hollow and meaningless if they are not prepared for some of the burning realities of the workspaces in which they will practice. My involvement with the movement may be limited, but the classroom remains a safe space to empower future educators to advocate for themselves, their students, and their education communities. Although it is challenging working in an environment where collective bargaining is not the norm, there is still hope based on some of the shared governance structures—at least at the school of education where I work—that one day, the entire university will be unionized.

As a K–12 teacher and union member from 2003 to 2021, one of the major challenges that the union had was ensuring that all colleagues in the field had the same rights as their traditional public schools' counterparts. Educator preparation programs do not discriminate on who they render services to or where those they will graduate will serve. Regardless of what biases or opinions some of us may have in relation to charter schools, they are not going anywhere anytime soon. It is therefore imperative that educators serving in these spaces have the same rights as their counterparts in traditional public schools. The gaps in compensation, job protections, and rights between traditional public school and charter school educators remain very wide, and past efforts to help unionize the latter have been thwarted at every step of the way by those at the top of charter management. I will continue to speak out and collaborate with other likeminded professionals to bring the plight of charter school educators to light and, it is hoped, work with organizers to integrate them into the labor movement. Parents and guardians have proven to be reliable allies when they are appropriately educated on the issues. My hope is that engaging underrepresented and inactive parent communities to serve as allies in both public schools and charter schools will help with charter school organizing efforts.

Looking forward, working with allies to increase the lobbying of policymakers to change their attitudes toward unions will constitute an area where I would like to devote my efforts. In the past, policymakers, including democratic lawmakers, have been strong advocates of standardized testing, which has not necessarily delivered on the promise of improving outcomes for students, especially those from historically underserved backgrounds. Unions and the communities coming together are helping to change the narrative on testing. For example, the state senate in New York voted 60-0, and the state assembly voted to eliminate standardized test scores from teachers' evaluations.

It is my hope that through my scholarship and continuous involvement with teachers' unions, I can help influence policy and mindsets on the true value of unions. Unions stand to benefit and build power through increased organizing efforts, cohesion among themselves, greater collaboration, and coalition building with partners and unlikely allies.

Solidarity forever!

Further Reading

American Federation of Teachers. (2025). *Protecting Our Students tool kit.* https://www.aft.org/sites/default/files/media/documents/2025/protecting_our_students_tookit_updated_0.pdf

Gibson, Britanny (2024). "Trump's Grip on the Union Rank and File." *Politico.*

Gonyea, D., & Inskeep, S. (2024). "The International Brotherhood of Teamsters is not endorsing a presidential candidate." *NPR News.*

Janus v. American Federation of State, County, and Municipal Employees, Council 31, 138 S. Ct. 2448. (2018).

Levitz, Eric (2019). "Unions Have Won the War of Ideas. Will That Win Them Power?" *New York Magazine.*

McMahon v. New York, 24A1203 (U.S. July 14, 2025). https://www.supremecourt.gov/opinions/24pdf/24a1203_poll.pdf

Roy, N. (2020). "National teachers union sues Education Secretary Betsy DeVos for repeal of student protections." *NBC News.*

Vela, H. (2025). "Miami-Dade teacher deported to Honduras after being detained at immigration check-up." NBC6 News South Florida.

ABOUT THE AUTHOR

Dr. Terence Ngwa is a veteran educator and organizational leader with over 20 years of national and international professional service and expertise. He has worked for many years to ensure an effective voice for educators, parents, and students in the K-12 setting. His work has successfully and repeatedly brought together education stakeholders to collaborate on improving outcomes for students, especially groups from historically marginalized backgrounds.

Dr. Ngwa earned a Bachelor's degree in French and English from the University of Yaoundé in his native Cameroon before emigrating to the United States. He has since served in various education roles in Washington DC as a middle school teacher, exchange student program coordinator, union representative, and ultimately, Washington Teachers' Union Executive Director. While serving in these roles, Dr. Ngwa earned a Masters Degree in educational leadership from Trinity Washington University, a Doctoral Degree in organizational leadership from Southeastern University, and certificates in Diversity and Inclusion and Collective Bargaining from Cornell University.

In 2021, Dr. Ngwa was selected to lead a new graduate level certificate program in school leadership in the School of Education at American University in Washington DC. He currently serves as a senior professorial lecturer and teaches various graduate level courses: Curriculum Design for the Classroom; School Improvement, Organization, and Administration; Collaborative Inquiry Through Systems Thinking; and Historical, Social, and Political Foundations of U.S. Education Systems. He also teaches Social Justice in Urban Education at the undergraduate level. Dr. Ngwa has designed and developed culturally responsive and inclusive content for school leadership preparation, supervised aspiring principals' internship experiences, and designed and led experiential learning exchanges to Europe and West Africa. He previously served as director of the Antiracist Administration, Supervision, and Leadership Certificate

Program and the International Training and Education Program within the School of Education. Dr. Ngwa is passionate about social justice, diversity, equity, and inclusion, and antiracist initiatives in education, and these are at the core of his commitment to education.

INDEX

P

R

Y